Yours, Mine and Hours

D0325101

Yours, Mine and Hours

Relationship Skills for Blended Families

John Penton and Shona Welsh

2007

Yours, Mine and Hours

Table of Contents

Acknowledgements

The authors gratefully acknowledge the work of the following authors and publishers who have kindly given their permission for the quotation or use of parts of their work in this book:

Corporate Coach U, for parts of Chapter Twelve including the concepts of *Asking Thought-Provoking Questions*, parts of *Becoming Comfortable with Silence*, and the *80-20* rule.

Inscape Publishing, for parts of Chapter Twelve including the DiSC® model.

Mindszenthy & Roberts Communications Counsel, for parts of the Communication Section, including Chapter Ten: the *WIFM Approach* and Chapter Eleven: *Creating a Family Pact*.

Random House Publishing, for the use of quotes from *Stepfamilies: Love, Marriage, and Parenting in the First Decade*. Bray, Dr. James H. and Kelly, John. New York: Broadway Books. 1998.

Prologue

Once upon a time in a galaxy far, far away...

No, this isn't some science fiction novel that tells the tale of exciting adventures on faraway planets. It is, however, a book about one of the most eventful and transforming experiences you can ever have —being part of a blended family. There *are*, however, many similarities between a science fiction plot and a blended family. Both feature, for example, a cast of aliens whose habits and attitudes are completely foreign to yours. Both involve experiencing some kind of conflict (not necessarily life or death in a blended family —although homicidal thoughts do occasionally arise). And both offer the opportunity to completely transform the way we view ourselves, our relationships, and even our world.

Another similarity between science fiction and blended families is there are very few instruction manuals or courses out there to help us navigate through unknown territory. Most of the time, we must fly by the seat of our pants, guessing moment to moment how best to handle new situations. Even though a significant percentage of American and Canadian families[1] are now living in blended family situations, the parenting models we grew up with, while a good basis from which to start, are often devoid of the wisdom and skills we need to survive and thrive in a blended family. That was certainly the case in our situation. We quickly realized that we were guessing our way on almost everything because neither of us had any framework whatsoever in understanding how to be successful stepparents —both of us have parents who have been together over forty-five years. Even if you did grow up in a blended family, you will often encounter new and different challenges you didn't anticipate.

Despite feeling we were quite realistic about the challenges involved in a blended family, we still suffered from a fair bit of naivety about what it would actually *mean*. In the years since that fateful decision, it has been a wild ride indeed. We have both learned a lot about what it is to establish a blended family, keep it going, and most importantly, how to survive as a couple through all of it. That's what brought us to the decision to write this book.

In the course of seeking advice for our family, we discovered some great sources of information on the nature of blended families. While the field of research is relatively young, there are some excellent studies that highlight the challenges and opportunities presented by blended families. However, it was never our intention to write a research-oriented book, nor did we anticipate it would be an exhaustive look at all the issues you will encounter in your blended family —others have already done a great job of that and their books, along with the research studies, are listed in the *Resources* section. Our simple intention was to write a user-friendly, easy-to-remember, practical book that focused specifically on the relationship aspects of blended families: first, the couple relationship within the family, and second, the relationship skills we see as crucial for the ultimate success of your blended family.

It is our hope that we can help other blended families by explaining some beliefs and tools that have worked for us. We certainly can't promise perfection or that all of it will work for you because every person, every couple, every family is unique. Some of you will already have experienced and dealt with the issues we address. In that case, we hope you will find confirmation of what you've been doing or get some new ideas about old situations. For others, some of this information may be completely new. In that case, we wish you much success in using the approaches that have worked so well for us, both from a marriage and a family perspective. If you don't find ideas about your particular situation in this book, consult the *Resources* and

References sections we have compiled in the back of the book and find it elsewhere. It matters not where you get the information, just as long as you get it.

No matter what you are facing in your blended family situation, one thing we can promise you is that it takes a lot of time and effort on the part of the parents — you — to help it all come together. That's why we've chosen the title *Yours, Mine, and Hours*. While it does take a lot of time at first, you will find your efforts will pay huge dividends the longer your blended family is together.

As we reflect on our blended family journey so far, we could never have anticipated how much we would learn in the years we have been together. As in those science fiction stories we mentioned earlier, we have learned how to live peacefully among aliens, resolve conflicts without bloodshed, and most importantly, positively influence how our children and we function in relationships. We wish the same for all of you as you learn to survive and thrive in your blended family.

John Penton and Shona Welsh

For our children Paul-Andrew, Tim, Rudie, Ryan and Kate.
Without them, none of this would have been possible.

Part 1

The Recipe for Blended Family Success®

Creating a family in this turbulent world is an act of faith, a wager that against all odds there will be a future, that love can last, that the heart can triumph against all adversities and even against the grinding wheel of time.[1]

- Dean Koontz
From the Corner of His Eye

Chapter One

What is the Recipe for Blended Family Success®?

Family isn't about whose blood you have. It's about who you care about.[1]

- Trey Parker and Matt Stone
South Park — Ike's Wee Wee, 1998

It was Christmas Day. We were enjoying a quiet, elegant dinner for two in a nearby resort town. John's three children were with their mother for the holidays, and Shona's son was with his father. Both of us were glad of the opportunity to steal away for a bit of alone time — a precious commodity when you have four children to deal with, whether or not they all live at home.

The wine steward served the wine with a flourish, and we clinked glasses in a toast to our new union   only six months old. It had been a tumultuous few years, both of us having endured stressful divorces as well as needing to overcome deeply ingrained cynicism about the opposite sex. Our partnership had grown slowly over the course of a year, neither of us willing to engage in any kind of serious relationship other than friendship. And then, when Shona accepted a job offer in a distant city, things went on fast-forward. In a three-week period we went from being very good friends to planning our life together. It just seemed natural. We have never looked back, and neither of us has ever been happier.

But that first Christmas dinner together sorely tried our relationship. As Shona took a sip of her wine, she felt a burning sensation all the way down her throat and into her stomach as the wine made its path through her body. While only an occasional drinker, she knew enough to figure out that this was not the usual way alcohol affected her. In fact, she knew enough to remember that the only time alcohol had *ever* affected her in exactly that way was when she was pregnant with her son.

Slowly, she put her glass down and looked across the table at John. "Ah, John?" she began tentatively, absolutely terrified at the thought that her suspicions might be true.

"Yes?" he answered innocently, unaware of the news that was about to change his life. It wasn't that he hadn't liked being a father —it was just that his kids were almost grown at that point, being fifteen, seventeen, and nineteen. And while Shona's son was only six, he spent every other weekend at his dad's, allowing us a regular bit of freedom to establish our partnership more fully.

"I believe I'm pregnant," Shona said, barely above a whisper.

John looked stunned for a moment. "Nah!" he replied. "Not possible." But the look on Shona's face made him hesitate. "What makes you think so?" This time it was his turn to whisper.

Shona explained the wine sensation.

John took a deep breath. "That would mean we'd have five kids…"

We looked at each other with what could only be described as sheer terror. Needless to say, we drank no more wine that night and spent the rest of the evening discussing what it would look like to have a new baby. John was forty-five at the time; Shona was thirty-five. It felt like a huge burden to start all over again, especially with the freedom we were beginning to have, given the ages of the kids and visitation schedules.

We both spent a relatively sleepless night waiting for morning when the stores would once again be open and we could confirm (or deny) our suspicions. When at last we sat together on our family room couch, both peering at the double blue lines indicating a positive pregnancy result, stunned silence was the best we could manage.

Since that day, many things have changed in our lives. We have a beautiful seven-year-old daughter, Shona's son is now thirteen, and John's three older children have all moved out and on to jobs and university. Life, while stressful at times, proceeds on a relatively smooth course, and we all have familiar routines we have negotiated and live by.

But the first two years were the toughest. They were marked by extreme fatigue, misunderstandings, resentments, conflicts, a few tears, and about 3,000 diapers. Blending a family of yours, mine, and then ours, took many, many hours. From the beginning, we had agreed as a couple that we would weather the storms of our blended family of two adults, five children, a bird, a puppy, and the occasional mouse together. It was fundamentally the best approach we could have taken.

Statistics will tell you that second marriages fail earlier and even more frequently than first marriages and the most important factor in these failures is children. This breakdown most often occurs within the first two years of remarriage. What you will read in this book is how we were determined our family would not become a statistic, and the approaches we adopted that have helped our relationship and our family not only survive but thrive. Eager not to fly by the seat of our pants, we drew on John's background in child development and supplemented that with our own research. Some theories we thought would work clearly did not; other relatively simply concepts worked like a charm.

There is also, we discovered, much good news about what we call the regenerative abilities of blended families. In his nine-year study of two hundred families through the Developmental Issues in StepFamilies (DIS) Research Project, clinical and family psychologist Dr. James Bray found that blended families can actually help heal the scars of divorce:

> ...*conventional wisdom has held that divorce permanently scars a child. [Although it is true] that a child is profoundly*

*affected by family dissolution…we found that a loving, well-
functioning stepfamily can help restore a youngster's sense
of emotional and psychological well-being. We also found
something else: A strong, stable stepfamily is as capable of
nurturing healthy development as a nuclear family. It can
imbue values, affirm limits and boundaries, and provide a
structure in which rules for living a moral and productive
life are made, transmitted, tested, rebelled against, and
ultimately affirmed.*[2]

What we will share with you in this book is an approach we
have used to do the things Dr. Bray has described, an approach
we have come to call the Recipe for Blended Family Success®.
We believe that if you use the Recipe ingredients —Marriage,
Acceptance, and Communication —you will experience much
success and happiness in your blended family life. It will make
the "hours" part of the "yours, mine, and hours" pass a lot more
easily.

The Recipe for Blended Family Success®

The Recipe for Blended Family Success® is a reflection
of everything we have learned in establishing and developing
our blended family. It has served us well in helping smooth the
bumpy patches and allowing us to experience peace, comfort,
and —yes! —even joy in our blended family. The Recipe for
Blended Family Success® centers on three main ingredients:
Marriage, Acceptance, and Communication. We like to think of
the first two —Marriage and Acceptance —as the philosophies
and attitudes to develop that will help get you through the living
day-to-day stuff —and the Communication stuff is the hands-
on, practical, what-you-can do stuff.

As you read through the descriptions of Marriage,
Acceptance, and Communication in this chapter and also in
further sections of this book, there will be some points you will
no doubt want to respond to with "yes, but…" To achieve clarity,
we have had to separate some of the issues. For example, we

briefly address male-female communications in the Marriage section, but go into it in a lot more detail in the Communication section. We ask you to stay with us because it all eventually comes together —but the three themes do significantly overlap each other.

Before we get started, there are a few issues around language usage we want to clarify. When we use the term "marriage," it is for simplicity only. It also applies in common-law relationships when you have chosen to become partners. We use the term marriage as a short form for couple relationship —please apply it to your common-law partnership the same as you would if you were formally married. In our case, we didn't actually get around to getting married until four years into our blended family, so many of the experiences you will read about happened before we were married.

We also want to clarify what we mean when we refer to blended families. We have noticed that some researchers distinguish between a stepfamily and a blended family; they define a stepfamily as one that lives with the children of only one parent, and refer to a blended family as one that incorporates children from both parents. For ease of discussion and understanding, we refer to both of these families as blended families, but everything applies even if you're living in a stepfamily versus a completely blended family.

Another language issue concerns distinguishing between families that have never been divorced and reformed, and a blended family. We have heard the never-divorced family referred to as a nuclear family, an intact family, an original family, a normal family, etc. We don't like the word "normal" because we believe normal is such a subjective term —what's normal for you might not be normal for us. Again, for ease of discussion, we have chosen to use the term "intact family" when referring to families that have never been through divorce. We don't mean to suggest that blended families are therefore not intact. In fact, we think they become incredibly intact once they've weathered the first few storms of figuring out who they are. It's just a decision we've made so we don't have to explain what we mean every time we're discussing an issue.

Ingredient #1: Marriage

When we give workshops about blended family skills, Marriage is the most controversial ingredient in our Recipe for Blended Family Success®. Specifically, it's not that anyone disagrees that looking after your marriage is an important blended family survival skill —it's just that we get a lot of gasps when we say that you must put your marriage *first* —*before* your children. If you find yourself gasping as you read this, bear with us for a moment.

Putting your marriage first in no way means your children are not a priority. It also does not mean you don't do everything as parents to give the children the best guidance, love, and support you can for a good start in life. What it does mean is that you attend to your relationship with your new spouse *as a primary means* of being the best parents you can be.

Anyone who has ever traveled on an airplane knows that, in the event of a change in cabin pressure, an oxygen mask will fall in front of you from the compartment above. Flight attendants emphasize that you must always put your mask on first before attempting to assist others (like the child in the seat next to you). The reasoning is that if you can't breathe, your efforts to help others will be hindered at best, fatal at worst.

The same is true of blended families. The parents must first be able to assist themselves in building a strong relationship before they can be of real assistance to their children. Divorce statistics for second marriages are painfully grim, and many couples we know cite stressors around stepchildren as being a key contributor to the failure of that marriage. Frankly, we think putting your marriage first is an excellent concept to keep in mind even for couples who live in an intact family. We'll explain why in more detail later.

It has been our personal experience, along with our observations of other blended families, that a key indicator of survival is the health, strength, and openness of the couple relationship. Simply put, if you can't build a strong, healthy marriage that exists outside your role of parenting, you can't build a strong, healthy blended family.

Key issues that we discuss in detail include:

- Why putting your marriage first is critical to the success of your blended family

- Understanding what you believe about and want out of marriage

- The differences between families that put their marriage first versus those that don't

- Understanding the foundations of a good marriage

    Why establishing and maintaining connection as a couple is critical and how having protected time and space supports that connection

- Why you need to craft a family vision and issues to consider in doing that.

There are no doubt other issues but these represent our key learnings about supporting our marriage in a blended family context.

Ingredient #2: Acceptance

The second ingredient in the Recipe for Blended Family Success® is the notion of Acceptance. What this means is that you are going to encounter a whole range of issues that you resist, come into conflict over, and plain just don't understand about the new spouse, the new children, and the new family. Some of them you may not even want to admit to yourself for they seem so small and petty. Trust us —it's the small and petty things that will get you first. Always keep in mind that it's okay to feel these things. (You are human, after all!) What matters is how you handle them.

Some of the issues we examine include:

- How good intentions for having a wonderful family aren't enough

- Common challenges for blended parents

- That guilt thing and how to manage it by not putting impossible standards on yourself

- Understanding that resisting all the issues is a waste of your time and energy, and that you must start with what you've got

- How to deal with all the fear, reaction, and worry living in a blended family brings out in you

- Learning the *Ten Laws of Acceptance* in a blended family and how they'll help you keep your sanity.

There are numerous issues we discovered in the complexity of our blended family, all of which we learned can begin to be solved by adopting an approach of Acceptance.

Notice that we said *begin* to be resolved. Acceptance is your *starting point* for moving ahead, not the cure-all for your numerous frustrations. In the words of The Borg Civilization in television's *Star Trek: The Next Generation,* "Resistance is futile." It is simply not worth your energy to resist, argue about, debate, and otherwise stew over many of these issues or other conflicts. Acceptance is an acquired skill, however, and not one that many of us come by naturally. It comes with a lot of hard work and attention, and develops over time.

Acceptance starts with an understanding on the part of both parents that the family will not be perfect. As strange as it may sound, many of us go into blended situations with starry-eyed notions that we'll be one big happy family. Part of that comes from your love for your new partner ("Together we can work anything out!"), and part of it comes from your genuine desire to be a good stepparent. Love and desire are certainly the best places to start, but they won't guarantee a smooth ride. It's Acceptance that will keep you moving forward.

Accept that the kids may not like you no matter what. Accept that you will have conflicts with the ex-spouse(s). Accept that the stepsiblings may not like each other. Accept that you are now responsible for more children. Accept that you may not love your new stepchildren, and that you may never love them. Accept that you have to share your time among the spouse, your children, and the stepchildren. Simply put, Acceptance ensures you will not get caught in a crisis of expectation where you expect things to turn out one way, and then are caught in a crisis when the situation turns out completely differently. Interestingly, this can affect you whether the results turn out more negatively *or* more positively than expected.

Ingredient #3: Communication

We know, we know —it's been overstated, overdone, overemphasized. You've heard it from your parents, your friends, and your boss until you're sick of hearing it. Nevertheless, you're going to hear it from us as well. Communication is, and always will be, one of your key tools in maintaining equilibrium in your blended family.

The Communication ingredient in the Recipe for Blended Family Success® is the practical, how to live day-to-day stuff. The Marriage and Acceptance issues are the attitudes and philosophies that will guide and support you as you live the Communication part, although we've offered you some tools in those two areas as well.

The key issues we discuss in communicating in your blended family are:

-   Understanding first and foremost how you communicate with each other as a couple

-   Managing the differences in male-female communications so you can be a team

-   Understanding the best way to get and hold your children's attention and deal with discipline and rewards

-   Understanding how to set boundaries for yourself as a parent

-   Using a variety of communication approaches to manage your blended family as well as build self-responsibility in your children

-   Using the concept of coaching to enhance communication

-   Understanding personality styles that influence how your blended family interacts.

One of the challenges of separating the topic of Communication from Marriage and Acceptance is that they tend to run together. Many of the issues we talk about under those first two categories have a lot to do with Communication. Our focus in the Communication section, however, is to provide you with some practical tools that can help you manage some of the challenging *general* communication situations you will encounter in your blended family. The tools presented in the Marriage and Acceptance sections *specifically* relate to those two topics.

⸎

That's the basic overview of the Recipe for Blended Family Success®. Like most things in life, the theory is simple, the reality much more challenging. Living in a blended family takes many hours of concentrated effort. So let's dive in and begin to make your day-to-day reality less challenging, if not less complicated...

Part 2

Ingredient #1: Marriage

Remarriage is the triumph of hope over experience.[1]
— Samuel Johnson

Chapter Two

Put Your Marriage First

Marriage is like wine. It is not properly judged until the second glass.[1]
　　　　Douglas William Jerrold

There is a very important reason why Marriage is the first ingredient in the Recipe for Blended Family Success® —it's because your marriage absolutely *has* to come first or the chances of success as a blended family are extremely slim. Dr. Bray's study found, in fact, that for many successful marriages within blended families, "at the heart of the family, there lay a very stable, satisfying marriage."[2]

Putting your marriage first may be a very tough message for many of you to hear, especially in our society where children are often the center of just about everything we do. If asserting that your marriage must always come first is offensive to you, we urge you to hear us out. We have seen so many blended families break up because the couple did not adhere to this fundamental principle. It has been the guiding light of our relationship, and sometimes the only thing we had to hang on to when things got tough.

Why put your marriage first?

Perhaps this particular learning has become so important to us to communicate to others because of our own previously unsuccessful marriages. While marriages break up for a variety of complex reasons, it has been our own personal experience that a huge problem arises when *all* of the time and energy of the couple is poured into the children. We have seen it in our own marriages as well as in the marriages of friends and family members: parents can often neglect each other in favor of the children. The result? The couple experience themselves as two strangers living together, eventually unable to remember why they got together in the first place. While we go into more detail on this topic a little later, we felt it was important to emphasize up front the repercussions of neglecting your marriage.

Those of us who have divorced (and particularly those of us who have divorced more than once) understand full well the tenuousness of the marital bond in today's society. In the past, societal structures helped keep many marriages together despite the problems. Today, marital relationships break down in much larger numbers basically because we understand there are alternatives to unhappy marriages, and we have the freedom to choose much more than our parents did. Not only that, because we have been through divorce once and actually survived, we know we could do it again. It's not that we want to; we just know it won't kill us. Precisely because it is so much easier to choose divorce nowadays, we believe that the issue of your marital relationship, now more than ever, must be uppermost in your mind to make a success of your blended family.

The fact is, if your marriage doesn't come first, the other two principles in the Recipe —Acceptance and Communication — really don't matter. If you don't put your marriage first, nothing else will work. This is consistent with what you will read in many self-help books: if you can't love and be happy with yourself, it's extremely difficult to love and be happy with others. Similarly, if you can't love and be happy in your couple relationship, it will be very challenging to extend love and happiness to your children.

Think about it this way. In deciding to blend your two families, your motivation, first and foremost, is your love for each other and your desire to be together. Your children, while a central factor in both of your lives, are *not* the reason you are blending the families in the first place. The two of you *are*. Becoming a couple and negotiating all the changes you both will need to make is, in and of itself, a difficult proposition. Adding each other's children to the mix makes it even more complicated, not to mention raising the stress level much higher than when it's only the two of you figuring out how you're going to live together. For this last reason alone, it is imperative that you and your partner are on the same page regarding your relationship and how you're going to manage the blended family situation.

We acknowledge that some people get remarried for reasons other than a love relationship with a partner. Some people have told us they remarried so they could have help with their children, finances, didn't want to be alone, etc. Every reason is individual, and while we personally don't recommend you enter into a blended family situation without a desire to forge a genuine love partnership with your spouse, we do recommend that, whatever your motivations, you need to have a rock solid relationship with your spouse or your chances for blended family success are slim.

Choosing to be a couple within a blended family is much different than choosing to be a couple when both of you are single, footloose, and fancy-free. Chances are one or both of you has been a single parent for a while, or perhaps you have always spent your parenting years as a single parent. Living with and raising your own children is challenge enough in itself, never mind being responsible for *someone else's* children. The behaviors, culture, traditions, and values the new family brings may be quite different than those of your family.

Added to this is the real possibility that you and your new partner have different parenting styles. To heap coals on an already roaring fire, you may not be particularly fond of the stepchildren, they of you, and the stepsiblings may prefer to be on a different planet than spend one day with each other in the same house. You're facing a vast array of complex situations, likes and dislikes, personal foibles, and conflicts to resolve, and that's with the children alone, never mind with each other.

You will both need an incredible amount of skill, patience and commitment to make it work. You're truly coming to term with yours (your partner's way of doing things), mine (your own way of doing things), and ours (how you will now do things together). You will unfailingly need to be each other's safe haven as well as each other's defender. As the old saying goes, "United we stand, divided we fall." Nowhere is that more true than for a marriage within a blended family.

Even more difficult is becoming a stepparent when you've never had any children of your own. The world of children can certainly seem strange and inhospitable to the uninitiated. Worse, if you find you disagree with the way your new partner has been parenting his or her child, the chances for conflict in your relationship just went up about a thousand notches. This becomes a particularly difficult issue if you decide to have children together because the issues that troubled you regarding your stepchild will come up again with your biological children.

In our professional lives, both of us have done a lot of work with issues of change and change management in organizations. One of the key principles of change all the experts agree on is that it is not actually the *change* itself that causes so much stress in people but rather the *transition* from the old way of doing things to the new way. William Bridges, a noted change expert, calls this period "The Neutral Zone."³ For you *Star Trek* fans out there, you may recall that the Neutral Zone is that area of space between the Romulan Empire and the Federation that neither side lays claim to, a place with no set rules where anything can happen and anything can be created, positive or negative.

The first couple of years in a blended family represent a Neutral Zone, a place where the past must be honored but largely released, and where the future must be conceived of and built. In this endeavor, the parents are the Change Transition Team —another necessary element of any successful change effort, according to the experts. If you and your spouse have a clear, joint vision that you are the anchor of the family (because your marriage comes first), you can be effective Change Managers, guiding all of your children through the Neutral Zone, even when you're not exactly sure yourselves where you're going.

What do you want from your marriage?

Before we go much further, it is important to identify what we are talking about in building a strong marriage within a blended family. When we urge you to put your marriage *first*, we are making an assumption that what you are looking for in a marriage is a *partnership*. We bring this up because we have observed a distinct tendency of human beings to form what we call transactional marriages —marriages where the couple view the union as an exchange of services, some kind of bargain where the man will do a certain set of things and the woman will do another set of things in return.

In the traditional example, the man will bring home most of the money, take care of all of the outdoor chores, and discipline the children. For her part, the woman will focus on maintaining the home, take care of all the domestic chores, and attend to the day-to-day care needs of the children. In more modern times, there are various combinations of who is responsible for what, but ultimately it comes down to a transaction where you get something for doing something else. These agreements can certainly be part of a good relationship but are, in our opinion, of secondary importance.

There's nothing wrong with this arrangement as long as both partners are happy with and agree to it. Unfortunately, these kinds of marriages can run into trouble as soon as one or both partners fail to live up to their side of the agreement for whatever reason —someone changes his or her mind about their priorities (the wife no longer wishes to stay home with the children, the husband decides he wants to stay home with the children), an event happens that changes the nature of the relationship (the man loses his job, the wife gets a promotion involving lots of travel), etc. In this game of I'll Trade You, when one person stops giving what was agreed upon, the marriage can often end. No person remains static, and as life moves on and serves up various challenges, we all grow and learn and change. The person you marry will undoubtedly not be the same person you'll be living with in five years. We actually think it's a miracle more people don't get divorced than is currently the case, for marriage is a constantly changing reality we must all continually redefine and rediscover.

We recently watched a television movie where a reporter was interviewing an elderly man about his life. When he mentioned his wife had died four years previously, the reporter commented that he must miss her. With a quizzical expression on his face, the man replied that he hadn't really thought about it. Surprised, the reporter said that surely he must have loved her because they had been together forty-five years. The man thought about it for a minute and responded, "Most people don't get married out of love, they get married out of *fear of not being loved.* That's why I got married."

Both of us were quite moved by this exchange, mainly because we recognized this motivation in our previous marriages. It's not that our ex-spouses were bad people —it's just that what we wanted was very different, and we also think that, at some deep level, we didn't want to live our lives alone. This doesn't mean we didn't love our ex-spouses, it just means that, given our genuine desire to have a partnership-oriented marriage, our transactional marriages faced a lot of struggles as the partners involved changed, grew, and evolved. The original transaction was not being lived up to or was never clearly discussed, so neither partner had a clear idea of how each saw his or her role. Somehow, we weren't able to adapt to the changes in the individuals in the marriage because we were stuck in the original agreement.

Shona's second marriage really underlines this changed agreement. When she and her ex-husband decided to have a child, they agreed that Shona would quit working and stay at home with their son. Unfortunately, a couple of unanticipated changes occurred to cause friction in this arrangement. First, Shona had always been a career-oriented person, and while she willingly gave up her career to care for her son, she discovered that her personality was not suited to being a stay-at-home mother for five or more years. While she loves her son as much as any mother, she found that she was bored, impatient, and craving adult company more than she had expected. Over time, she realized she would be a more attentive, patient, and happy mother by continuing to have a work life of her own outside of the home. When her son was six months old, she returned to part-time work.

Her husband had not anticipated Shona's change of heart. While he willingly agreed to Shona returning to work, he seemed unprepared for the change in the housework/cooking/child care situations that would bring. Over time, Shona began to feel she was carrying the full load of housework and child care on top of her career (which became full-time again when her son turned two). In fairness, Shona admits they never fully discussed each other's view of child care, what would be an equitable division of housework, etc. before they found themselves in conflict. In the end, Shona refused to have any more children because she felt there was no way she could handle any more work.

While the marriage finally ended for a variety of reasons, Shona believed she had been living the life of a single parent for quite some time without actually being single — assuming all the housework, child care, and financial duties. (Her husband had been unemployed for quite a while when they divorced.) Mainly, this perception was based on the fact that she expected her husband to share in half the duties and was disillusioned when it didn't happen. For his part, Shona believes her ex-husband saw their marriage in more traditional terms, where Shona would be responsible for children and home, and he would be responsible for providing financially and going out to work. Neither view of marriage is wrong, it's just that they never really got to the root of each other's view (or even really knew themselves what each other's view was), and when the terms changed (in each other's opinion), the marriage suffered.

Unfortunately, we believe most of us are not aware of our mental models of marriage until we're well into the relationship, nor do we openly discuss these models. Husbands and wives are caught in a time when old social structures governing roles in marriage are melting away, and they're not really sure what the new roles look like. One glaring example of the changing social rules around what marriages look like is the issue of gay marriage. It confounds society because it doesn't fit in the box we have all created around marriage. It challenges us to reflect on our definition of marriage, and later, family.

In any marriage, it's not unusual to begin patterning your marriage on how your parents did it, only to find that doesn't work for you. That's when the conflict happens — the unspoken agreement between you and your spouse changes regarding roles, and one or both of you feel let down. Obviously, getting clear about what marriage means to you is a key first step when you're discussing marriage.

What does marriage mean to you?

We believe most people would choose to have a partnership-oriented marriage rather than a transaction-oriented marriage —whatever that looks like for individual couples (it could be traditional, it could be more modern). One of the reasons the divorce rate has soared around the world is the fact that rigid social structures requiring us to marry for life are no longer in force and we are free to end marriages that don't fulfill our needs and make us happy —and a significant percentage of us are doing just that. In other words, more of us are seeking out relationships that will allow us to be the full person we are while merging our life interdependently (not dependently) with another person, which is what defines a true partnership in the first place.

This does not suggest in any way that your current marriage, if transactional, cannot evolve into something completely different (we think the Recipe is one way to effect that transformation), nor are we suggesting that you rush out and get divorced because you have recognized transactions or fear of being alone/not loved characteristics in your marriage. We simply want to point out that your best chance of success in a marriage within a blended family (and indeed within an intact family) is to attend to building a partnership within your marriage *first*, and then jointly deciding how you will guide your family and your children as a team. In a mainly transactional marriage, it may be quite difficult to learn to put your marriage first above all other things because both of you are used to focusing on something other than the two of you as the reason for being —usually children —but we believe it can be done.

Dr. Bray's findings support our experience that establishing a strong marital relationship is critical to the health of your blended family. In fact, he concluded from his study that a strong blended family marriage has three foundations:

> *First, the husband and wife have to attend to their adult needs —to nurture their relationship. Second, they need to develop a shared vision of marriage and family life. Third, they have to develop a consensus on parenting and other child-related issues.*[4]

We'll talk about shared vision and a consensus on parenting in more detail later.

What it looks like when your marriage doesn't come first

Whatever your situation, there are all kinds of problematic issues that arise when the marriage is put second to the children in a blended family. Here are a few examples we have witnessed. (Please note all names and some minor details have been changed to protect privacy.)

Richard and Gail

When Richard and Gail first got together, they were deliriously happy. Gail had just finished a college degree after having two daughters right out of high school. As a student and a single parent, she had had a rough few years, but now her daughters were eight and ten, and she had just married Richard, a once-divorced successful professional with no children. For his part, Richard was quite willing to take on responsibility for parenting Gail's two young daughters. Their father had long since disappeared from their lives, and very quickly both girls were referring to Richard as Dad. The future looked bright.

As the girls grew, however, Richard and Gail began to run into serious conflict. Every time there was a dispute in the house while Gail was out, Richard would solve the problem in the way he thought best. When Gail arrived home, she would often feel his decision had been too strict or punitive and would reverse his decision in favor of a softer approach. The more she did this, the more she put their marriage in jeopardy. Richard came to feel like he was just a wallet — that he was good enough to provide financially for the girls (and did so willingly and generously), but obviously not good enough to serve as a genuine father with all the decisions that entailed. He and Gail ended up in many fights over disciplining the girls, with him complaining about being powerless and her feeling like he had no right to make disciplinary decisions about *her* daughters.

After eight years of that kind of interaction, Richard and Gail's relationship had deteriorated to the point where he had completely given up even talking to her about the girls' behavior. By then they had had so many struggles over the girls that Gail didn't respect Richard and finally decided to end their marriage.

Essentially, their marriage ended over a series of power and trust issues that had the potential to be resolved if they had dealt with them openly and honestly. Gail always put her daughters first, which inevitably left Richard feeling left out, disrespected, and powerless. Since their divorce, they have both remarried and are both living in yet another blended family situation.

Debbie and Donald

This couple never did make it into an actual blended family situation because Donald and Debbie could never reach any kind of agreement about either parenting or relationship styles. It's not that they didn't love each other; it's just that Donald could never get Debbie to take some time for herself or the two of them as a couple.

When Debbie and Donald met, Debbie had been a single parent raising three children for several years, while Donald's kids had grown up and moved out. Debbie was also working toward an advanced degree and was extremely busy. And that's where the problems began. Donald noticed that whenever he and Debbie were together, she would complain bitterly about never having any time to herself. He began to take note of exactly what Debbie did with her spare time, and he realized that she spent every spare moment catering to her kids. It's not that he thought she shouldn't take her kids to activities or help them with schoolwork, it's just that she was doing many things that he felt weren't necessary. Sure those things made her kids' lives very comfortable, but it was exhausting Debbie, making her resentful and short-tempered. She had no real time left over to put any energy into building her relationship with Donald or pursuing any of her own interests.

After their relationship was well established and quite serious, Donald made a few suggestions. Perhaps Debbie could attend two of her son's weekly baseball games instead of all four. Perhaps she could drop off her daughter at her swimming lesson and pick her up afterward instead of sitting at the pool the entire time waiting for her. Perhaps she could assign specific daily or weekly chores to each child to lighten her load and at the same time teach each child a sense of responsibility and contribution to the family. Given that the children were all over the age of ten, Donald felt it wasn't unreasonable for Debbie to give them more responsibility and teach them she had a life of her own. Debbie was consistently unwilling to try Donald's suggestions because she had a rigid model of parenting she was unwilling to examine.

Once her children became teenagers, she began experiencing a whole range of behavior and other serious problems with them and frequently asked Donald for his advice. Despite his best efforts, she still disregarded everything Donald suggested and seemed more willing to live with the frustration and anguish the children's behavior caused than deal with it. Donald came to see it as weak parenting, where Debbie would not make the tough decisions that parents must sometimes make because she felt bad about punishing her children.

For several years, Debbie was convinced that the best solution was for Donald to move in and help her, both financially and with disciplining the children; she constantly tried to talk him into it. Donald had grave misgivings about doing that, and they had many discussions about the changes Debbie would need to consider if a live-in partnership were to succeed. Donald was willing to take a chance and proposed the next Christmas. Within five months, their engagement ended; Debbie was simply not willing to entertain some of the changes with her children Donald felt needed to occur to get the family and their relationship running smoothly.

Cheryl and David

When Cheryl and David got married, Cheryl was thrilled to have finally found her soul mate. Married very briefly once before, she had waited a long time to meet someone as wonderful as David. Cheryl did not have any children but David had a ten-year-old son who lived with him during the week. She enjoyed David's son and had no reservations about the three of them becoming a blended family.

The first year of their marriage, however, was a tough one. Living with David and his son was quite different than Cheryl had imagined. She thought David let his son get away with all kinds of bad behavior from table manners to how he reacted when he was told no. For example, he would tell his son that he would go to his room if he didn't stop whatever he was doing. His son would continue his behaviour, David would repeat the promise of punishment, and again, his son would continue. All David ever did was repeat the promise of punishment but he never actually followed through with it. Cheryl could see that

David's son didn't believe a word he said and knew that no punishment would ever be enacted. This allowed him free rein to behave in whichever way he chose.

Over time, she became quite uncomfortable and distressed around the boy and began dreading coming home from work because she never knew what kind of annoying behavior she would have to deal with that night. She talked to David numerous times about the issue, but he was never willing to change what he was doing.

Cheryl often felt David believed she didn't have a right to say too much about how he parented his son because he wasn't hers. In frustration, Cheryl took to staying in her bedroom every night after dinner. She told David it was because she had lots of homework to do as she was working toward a degree, but mostly it was just to avoid being around the boy and witnessing David's ineffective attempts to discipline him. She felt very much like she and David were at a stalemate and worried for their marriage. Worse, she had always wanted a child of her own and she and David had been discussing having a baby. Given his parenting style, however, Cheryl knew that having a baby would be a bad decision, and she was quite distraught over having to forget about having her own child because her husband wouldn't discuss parenting styles with her.

When she became pregnant totally by accident, Cheryl worried about their future while David was delighted at the prospect of a baby. They have yet to sit down and discuss parenting styles, even though the baby has now arrived.

Anita

While she isn't in a blended family situation, Anita is a composite of many single mothers we know: they won't commit to any number of good men they have dated because they have developed an emotional life centered on their children. Shona believes she also fell into this trap when she became a single parent, putting a great deal of her emotional energy into her son.

Anita had been a single parent for seven years. Though he was in the fifth grade, her son still slept with his mom in her bed most nights. She was also quite indulgent of his behavior, allowing him to refuse to eat dinner if he didn't feel like it, letting him eat all the junk food he wanted, buying him all the latest computer games the minute they came out, and signing him up for every activity he showed the slightest passing interest in.

She didn't take phone calls from friends at night during the week because she devoted all of her evening time to her son. Most days and weekends she spent running him to various activities. If her son made a commitment at school and then decided he didn't want to do it, she'd support his decision. She rarely accepted invitations from friends to go out because she felt hiring a babysitter would be abandoning her son. In short, she wanted to give her son everything she never had, protect him from all the hurts she had to go through as a child, and ensure that he grew up feeling loved and nurtured.

It's not that these were bad motivations. The problem was that Anita had no life for herself. Everything she did revolved around her son. Any man she dated had to pass muster with the boy, and while he wasn't outright hostile, he made it clear that he'd rather have Mom to himself. Once, when she became serious about a man who had a son of his own, her son made life so miserable by fighting with the boy every time they were together, that she ended the very promising relationship because the kids just couldn't get along. According to Anita, she could never be happy if her son wasn't happy.

On the few occasions her son visited his dad, she would cry when he left and miss him terribly the whole time he was gone, relieved when he finally returned. While she had clearly set it up to guarantee she could not make a relationship work, she would become depressed at not having a partner in her life and was acutely aware that she was getting older every year. More than anything, she said, she wanted a partner to share her life with.

In this situation, there is a disconnect between what Anita sees as effective parenting and how the rest of the world sees it. Because she has been alone with her son so long, she has come to depend on him and their relationship to meet her emotional needs. One friend's mother commented, after meeting Anita and her son, "She needs to get straight that she's his mother, not his buddy," and was quite appalled to hear that Anita often had her son sleep with her so she wouldn't be alone. This situation is going to make it difficult for Anita to form any kind of bond with a man until she learns to separate her own, adult emotional life from that of her child.

❧

In some of these situations there was a distinct disconnect between the man and the woman regarding how to deal with the children. Many times when a conflict arose, the birth parent would err on the side of defending or doing for the children, which left the new partner out in the cold. This is just as problematic in an intact family as it is in a blended family; however the divisions are often a lot more stark in a blended family than in a traditional nuclear family. It can be very easy to defend yours in the face of theirs, resisting or complaining about behavior. The minute one spouse does that, however, the marriage is in jeopardy.

Another element that might present a challenge is the birth parent's belief that no one can parent his or her kids the way he or she can. Some might even be fearful of the evil stepparent syndrome —real or imagined —and feel they have to protect their children from the new spouse. Again, this is a serious issue for your marriage because it speaks to an underlying lack of trust.

As in all marriages, a united front is critical to maintain harmony, discipline, and structure, or one of the parents inevitably becomes impotent in the eyes of the children (if you can even get as far as becoming a stepparent). When that happens, it's not long before the spouse begins to view the stepparent as impotent as well, and the relationship suffers. If you can set the parenting rules *together* ahead of time, negotiate what you both can live with, and then actually live what you have agreed to, there is very little need for either parent to go into defensive mode. This negotiation about parenting is all part of putting your marriage first, even though it focuses mainly on the children. After all, when you decide something together, you are strengthening and valuing your marriage. Later on, we'll discuss parenting styles and agreements in more detail.

What it looks like when your marriage comes first

There are numerous books out there discussing what makes a marriage work. We've read many of them and have yet to find the 'one right way', the best formula for making your marriage successful. Generally speaking, however, it all comes down to this: treat each other with kindness and respect.

Marriage in a blended family is no different. It's just a little more complicated because you've got more players with an interest in the game. Here are a few things we have found serve us well in maintaining and nurturing a happy marriage in a blended family.

Loyalty to spouse first

As animals, we are naturally hard-wired to defend our own, and nowhere does this have the potential for volatility more than a parent defending his or her child. But the thing that separates humans from the rest of the animal kingdom is our ability to reason as well as exert self-control. There were many times at the beginning of our blended family that one or both of us had to force ourselves to bite our tongues in the face of the other spouse doing something with or saying something to our biological children with which we didn't agree.

We cannot emphasize this tongue-biting enough. The moment conflict is happening with the children is *not* the time to take up the issue with your spouse. To do so undermines your spouse's authority as a parent figure in the house, something that has to exist for your blended family to function smoothly. In the early days of your blended family this is particularly important because that's the time you will be carefully trying to build and establish that role for your spouse. If you openly argue and question his or her decision, the children will have no reason to respect their stepparent's judgment; they will know they can just get you to reverse it later. This applies equally with younger and older children. While you will probably pay a more direct disciplinary role with younger children, teenagers still need to understand that authority in the house rests with the adults, biological parents or not.

Your child will not be permanently scarred to have to endure, for a few hours, the discipline your spouse has meted out. If you truly believe it is unfair or wrong, wait until the children have left the room or find an opportunity to speak with your spouse out of earshot. Explain your opinions and feelings calmly and with respect and, chances are, your spouse will be able to discuss the situation calmly as well.

Both of us have overreacted with the other's children from time to time, and our commitment to remain unfailingly loyal to each other in front of the children has done wonders for our faith and trust in each other. There have been times when the children deserved an apology, which was duly delivered by whichever spouse was in the wrong. In every situation, this opportunity to apologize and right a wrong with a child has allowed us to model to him or her that adults can make mistakes and admit their errors. So while you're busy building communication and understanding in your marriage, you're also building a mature, respectful relationship with the children.

This pattern of supporting your spouse in front of the children, even if you disagree with the specific approach he or she took, does not refer to any situation where physical or emotional abuse is involved. That's a completely different case, of course, and must be addressed with quite a different response. Any situation where excessive physical force is used is unacceptable (it may well be appropriate to physically escort a young child to his or her room) and belittling children is an equally unacceptable approach to problem-solving.

Trust and faith in intention

Having loyalty to your spouse in front of the children takes trust and faith. In turn, having trust and faith in your spouse will create more loyalty. While your spouse may not always handle situations with you or the children as well as he or she could, it's critical to remember that *you love each other.* You may fumble and offend at times, but underneath all of it is that pivotal emotion.

All of us need to learn how to behave in any relationship, couple or blended family. Sure, we bring experience from other relationships, but everyone is unique and you can't impose a cookie-cutter approach to getting along. Each of us is a flawed human being just trying to navigate this complicated thing called life. If we remember the basic intention is to love each other, it become a lot easier to overlook each other's missteps, foibles, and sometimes infuriating habits. Many parts of this book address this concept directly, so we won't belabor it here.

Making time for each other

We talk about this issue in Chapter Four in a lot more detail, but it's worth mentioning here as well. Ensuring that you have regular, daily times to connect with each other as a couple is critical to the health of your relationship. You are surrounded by children, ex-spouses, and complicated situations every day in a blended family. You need to constantly remind yourselves why you're dealing with all of this in the first place — to be together. This is not optional. As you'll read later, we've discovered that it takes about seven days of not connecting with each other to begin drifting apart. A good marriage doesn't necessarily take hard slogging work but it does take consistent attention.

One quick example of this is when both of us travel. Given the nature of our business, one of us is out of town at least once per month. But no matter where we are, we phone each other every night, even if we're only away one night. If one of us is halfway around the world and the time difference is measured in many hours, then we send e-mails back and forth. Sometimes we have absolutely nothing to say to each other besides 'hi' and 'I'm doing fine'. It doesn't matter. It's not about the content of the conversation, it's about the connection. We feel like we're in tune with each other on a daily basis.

Openness to listen

Being the couple at the head of a blended family is one of the toughest roles you will play in your life. It is not the place to allow your ego to get the better of your good judgment. Sometimes you will be wrong. Sometimes you will overact. So what? The mark of any successful marriage is not what you do when things go right, but what you do when things go wrong. And listening plays a big part in resolving issues.

Many studies we have read on listening indicate that it is the least-developed of all communication skills. We get formal instruction on reading, writing and speaking in school, but very few of us learn how to be better listeners.

Effective listening can be very complicated, but the heart of it is actually quite simple. Be willing to put aside your own agenda, opinions, ego, beliefs, and experiences and truly hear what your spouse is saying to you. You may not agree with him or her but you will have a much better understanding of what's important to him or her. In the end, your opinion of their reaction and feelings is irrelevant. You still need to respect that they feel that way and that it's real for them.

One of our former spouses used to dismiss certain topics that were raised, saying "They're not a problem for me". Maybe not. But if one spouse has a problem with something in a marriage then there's a problem. Period. Unwillingness to listen to and understand it doesn't make it go away, it just makes it go underground. And it will most certainly grow and fester before emerging as a much bigger issue later on.

Willingness to change your mind

After you've done all that listening, you have to be willing to change your mind. There's nothing wrong with reversing a decision or a perspective. In fact, the ability to change your mind is a primary way you can build trust and faith in your spouse. If he or she believes you're willing to listen and adjust your perspective, your chances of being happy together and having even better communication next time increase exponentially.

Willingness to admit you're wrong

We once heard a parenting expert say that the greatest single thing a parent can do to raise self-esteem in children is to say "I was wrong". We also think it's one of the best things you can do in your couple relationship. It's hard on our egos, but being able to admit we're wrong is another thing that builds trust and faith in our spouse. No one likes to feel like there's a set of hard and fast rules that govern our relationships and our lives. Admitting you're wrong does require a certain vulnerability on your part, but again, vulnerability is based on the amount of trust and faith you're willing to put in your spouse. Have trust and faith that they will not take advantage of your error and commit to doing the same for them.

Willingness to change

As we've already discussed, when someone changes in a relationship, it can cause upheaval because the 'rules' under which both of you were operating have shifted. We need to be willing to change when the situation demands it. Sometimes it feels very threatening but that doesn't make it any less necessary. Your willingness to change when the situation requires it will be helped by your ability to practice the six preceding elements of what it looks like when you put your marriage first.

One example of this is when John decided he wanted to quit his job and work with Shona. Shona had left a job to open her own business, and part of what helped her feel less anxious about it was the fact that John had a job; she felt like the family still had a financial safety net. He loved his job and was very challenged by it and she did not foresee that situation changing.

But change it did. Just over a year after Shona started her business, John encountered some health issues that, along with some organizational changes, caused him to want to leave his steady employment. He wanted to work with Shona in her business instead.

This threw Shona into a tailspin and all her fears of not being able to feed the children, pay the mortgage, and basically survive came to the forefront. Additionally, she was somewhat anxious about the effect working together every day would have on the marriage. We had many conversations over several months to address her fears. In the end, it came down to a leap of faith for Shona. After coming to the conclusion that very few things in life are irreversible, Shona agreed to John's quitting. If it didn't work out, we'd figure out how to solve it. It turned out to be the best decision we could have made, but it sure didn't feel like it to Shona at the beginning.

Willingness to forgive and forget

Your willingness to forgive your spouse's transgressions has a lot to do with the trust and faith you have in his or her intention. If you keep their good intentions in the forefront of your mind, even when you're infuriated with them, it won't diminish your anger in the moment but it will allow you to let it go without lingering bad feeling.

One thing that aggravates Shona about John is a tendency to leave things lying around. This is particularly annoying in the kitchen. John is the main cook in the family, and in the course of creating many wonderful culinary delights, the kitchen is invariably the victim. A swath of pots, pans, cooking utensils and vegetable peelings are a regular feature. John is not a 'clean as you go' cook. He's more of a 'creative chaos' cook. While the results are amazing, the carnage left behind is sometimes overwhelming.

But whenever Shona finds herself getting fed up with the mess, she remembers two things. The first thing is that John is not an emotionally demonstrative person. Being somewhat quiet and reserved, his gourmet efforts are one of the key ways he shows love and devotion to Shona and the family. We eat better every day than most customers of five-star restaurants. While she might not like the mess, Shona understands that John's cooking is an act of love. It sounds cheesy, but it really is true. Just thinking about it while she cleans the kitchen is usually enough to dispel any lingering anger she has.

The second thing she remembers when infuriated with John is gratitude. Having been through two unsuccessful and heart-wrenching marriages, she waited a long time to find John. If he were dead and gone tomorrow, she would give anything to have him back messing up the kitchen. If the first approach doesn't work, this one always does.

Forgiving and forgetting has a lot to do with the perspective you choose to live by. You can let every little thing get to you and forget the big picture of being in a loving, satisfying relationship, or you can appreciate and be grateful for all the great intentions behind the issue that's infuriating you.

Transparency

This concept rolls a lot of what we've already mentioned into one, broad category. Transparency is something we try to live by not only in our couple relationship but also with the children. Simply put, it reflects a sincere desire to be honest about your feelings, the situation, and to provide an explanation for your behavior. It's a powerful concept because it requires that you justify your behavior to *yourself* before trying to do so with someone else. It allows you the opportunity to self-evaluate (always tough) to ensure you are not merely acting on patterned behavior or emotion that you haven't thought through. It's a personal accountability mechanism that allows you to think very clearly and carefully about your own motivations.

On one occasion, for example, Shona 'lost it' over a broken dinner plate. One of John's children had broken it, and her reaction seemed all out of proportion to him. He was genuinely perplexed and asked Shona why she was so upset about a broken dinner plate. Shona didn't really know herself so she said she wanted to think about it for a while.

After a couple of hours, she realized that it wasn't the dinner plate she was reacting to. It was having all of her dutifully cared-for things handled with what she saw as disregard. As we'll see later, one of the challenging issues a stepparent often experiences is getting used to children handling your things when you've never had to share them before. There had been several incidents of broken items that month, all at the hands of John's children, all of which Shona had handled relatively calmly. But the dinner plate was the last straw, and after reflecting on her behavior, she realized she had a deeply-held resentment of having to surrender her possessions to the inattention of those who hadn't worked to buy them.

A more complete understanding of her own behavior allowed her to discuss the situation with John calmly and allowed John to have a full understanding of what, on the surface, appeared to be a minor incident.

෴

It is a reality that the above approaches, while useful in any couple relationship, become even more important when you're a couple in a blended family. Many of the issues you will find yourselves dealing with together will have to do with the children, not just the two of you. Sometimes, the issues will overlap so much that you will find it difficult to separate the 'children issues' from the 'couple issues'.

We're going to talk in more detail later about the communication and behavioral techniques that will help you navigate the conflicts inherent in a blended family, some of which we've already touched on in this chapter. In the meantime, however, we wanted to be sure our message of putting your marriage first was clear. If you're still in doubt, read on to the next chapter for more perspective on the importance of your marriage.

Chapter Three

The Four Pillars of Marital Success

Example is not the main thing in influencing others. It is the only thing.[1]

- Albert Schweitzer

I f we haven't yet convinced you that putting your marriage first is essential to making a success of your blended family, we want to remind you of and also help you reflect on some realities of marriage and family life.

1. Your children's job is to grow up and leave you

Intact family couples and blended family couples alike have the same challenge — forging and maintaining a life of their own that is separate from their children. In an intact family, couples are often fortunate in that they had a chance to be alone as partners before the children arrived. Blended families don't have that luxury, so it's doubly important that couples work at developing their own joint and separate lives and interests apart from the children.

Children's primary responsibility is to grow up, leave home, and become adults. People spend the vast majority of their lives as adults, not children, and we believe our number one job as parents is to guide our children in becoming happy, fulfilled, compassionate, considerate, and contributing adults. Because of this, we are deeply disturbed by the current trend to build *everything* a family does around the children — their wants and needs, their likes and dislikes. While you should always take your children's wants, needs, likes, and dislikes into consideration, it is also important to realize that children need to aspire to live in the adult world. Building all your family activities and interests around them creates a false environment inconsistent with what they will experience in the outside world, and often seriously erodes a couple's ability to spend time alone or develop joint adult interests.

Please don't misunderstand us. You should and must be available to your children in ways appropriate to their age as they grow. Obviously, the kind of time and attention you give your fourteen-year-old will be vastly different than the kind of time and attention with which you approach your two-year-old. Nonetheless, you are a separate person from your children and have your own life to live. The trick in doing this is to set appropriate boundaries.

Children know no boundaries and will keep taking, taking, as long as you let them — it's their job. They are not yet sophisticated enough to understand that a relationship isn't a one-way street. A perfect example of this in our house is no matter how much time we have spent with the younger children on a given day (the amusement park, swimming, just hanging out), they will almost always insist on more, using every emotional blackmail technique they know (pouting, crying, clinging) to get us to acquiesce. Your children need to understand there are limits to everything, and you are *not* being a bad parent when you sometimes say no.

Women tend to struggle with this more than men. A few years ago, Shona had a book she wanted to read, but four-year-old Kate wanted to watch a cartoon with Mom. Shona agreed, but half an hour later when the cartoon was over, she picked up her book as Kate began watching one of her children's movies. She asked if Mom could stay in the room with her and read while she watched the movie and Shona agreed. Ten minutes into the movie, Kate was crawling all over Shona and trying to grab her book away from her, insisting that Mom watch the movie too.

It was emotionally difficult for Shona to say no (we all want our kids to be happy), but she also recognized that she had already set boundaries for Kate. Giving in to Kate's pressure tactics would teach her that Mom didn't really mean what she said, and it would also cause Shona to feel cheated out of reading a good book she had been looking forward to. Insisting on having our own needs met —as individuals as well as a couple —will teach our children how to respect those needs as well as develop a confident and respectful ability to set their own boundaries later in their own lives.

More importantly, if you invest all of your energy in your children, you will inevitably find yourself living with a stranger twenty or so years later. Many midlife crises happen when the kids are nearly grown or have moved out and husbands and wives start questioning their lives and relationships, realizing that half their lives are gone. Research shows that divorce rates spike when children leave home. Between 1981 and 1991, divorce rates for couples married thirty years or more increased by sixteen percent in the United States.[2] The American experience shows that marriages do come under pressure when children are no longer the center of the relationship. Marriage experts say that parents can be so busy with all that's involved in raising their children day to day —not to mention attending to their own careers —that their own relationship problems may go unrecognized.[3] In the words of American playwright Lillian Hellman, "People change and forget to tell each other."[4]

A case in point is one couple we know who have four children. Putting your marriage first means getting the heck away from your kids sometimes, and this couple refuses to leave their kids alone or be very far away at any time. One Saturday night, we offered to have all four children for a sleepover so the two of them could have a date. In the years we had known them, we had never once seen them alone together, either at home or out. Most often, they would do the tag team parenting thing, where one parent would be home with the children while the other parent was out doing whatever, and then they would switch. We were quite excited for them, wondering what they would do. Would they go out for dinner? To a movie? To a nearby resort town for a bed and breakfast getaway? As it turned out, they didn't do any of these things —or anything else for that matter. In the end, they were so self-trained to attend to the needs of their children before their needs as a couple that they couldn't bring themselves to go out. They stayed home to be close to the phone just in case one of the kids needed them.

Sad to say, this couple has continued that pattern, and most of the time they both look stressed and tired. We wonder what the future holds for them as their children grow up, leave home, and they are left with just the two of them again. Do you suppose they will even remember how to *be* a couple planning romantic dinners or warm, sultry vacations? We fundamentally believe that if you don't remember your reason for being together as just the two of you, you will find yourself wondering what happened to that person you had known and loved all those years ago. It can be very lonely and very distressing.

Pouring all of your time, energy, and attention into your children is, in our opinion, a really good way to ensure you will face this kind of marital discord later in life, a time when you most want to be enjoying life together in a close marriage, free of the responsibilities children bring. Always remember that your children have their own lives and you have yours. Your job is to guide them for a while and then set them free, all the while never relinquishing your own identity and your own path. You have your own life challenges to contend with. Teach them as best you can and then let them go. You cannot learn or live your life for another person, and this is particularly worth remembering when it comes to your children (it can often be tempting). They have their own paths to follow. We repeat—you are *not* your children. You are a person in your own right. Never forget your identity.

2. *Your own good marriage is a gift to your children*

Modeling good relationships post-divorce is one of the best gifts you can give your children, biological and step. While

John's first marriage was not a horrible existence for his three older children, it was also true that a loving marital relationship did not exist for quite some time. You can't model what you don't have. Therefore, John believes his children didn't have a positive view of what a close relationship could be between a man and a woman. There wasn't a lot of screaming, anger or bitterness in his first marriage, but there also wasn't a lot of closeness and love. Particularly with regard to his daughter, who spent the most time with us in our blended family, John felt good that she could witness our close marital bond. In fact, she made pointed comments on numerous occasions on the closeness we had between us and the lack of stress in the house because of it.

Shona echoes the same sentiment about her second marriage. There weren't nights filled with arguments or raised voices, but she also doesn't feel her son was witnessing the truly close partnership marriage could be. Both of us have many adult friends who knew years ago that their parents weren't happy and shouldn't be together, but their parents stayed together nonetheless. Almost all of them report difficulties in their own partner relationships and ascribe them to never having learned what a positive, loving, functional relationship looked like.

For us, this experience of being able to model a better relationship in a blended family is a great argument for not staying together because of the children. Many couples express the view that they would rather not cause their children trauma through divorce and therefore sacrifice their own need for a loving, close partnership in the misguided impression it will be better for the children. The truth is, it doesn't matter what age your children are when you get divorced —it is painful and distressing no matter what. We hope this is somewhat comforting to those of you who are still feeling guilty that your divorce/break-up has somehow permanently damaged your children. Please don't get us wrong —we are certainly not advocating for divorce. Both us believe that the ideal is always an intact first marriage and family. But we don't live in an ideal world, and life certainly doesn't always turn out the way we planned.

Members of the Adult Kids of Divorce (AKOD) club on www.yahoo.com can attest to the pain their parents' divorce caused them. All eighteen years or older when their parents divorced, many confirm that their parents' divorce was just as traumatic for them as adults as it would have been as children. Club cofounder Susan Cherepon says the 1999 divorce of her parents after twenty-five years of marriage was "absolutely the worst thing that ever happened to me, bar none. It rips your whole world apart. Everything you thought you were sure of, suddenly you're not sure of."

Susan Hackett, whose parents divorced when she was in graduate school, agrees: "It was a terrible time. I went through all the pain and grief that any child does when this sort of thing happens, but I had the added bonus of having zero support because I was an adult."

Mandy Hagood, twenty-five at the time of her parents' divorce, emphasizes that it's never a good time, but does wonder if it would have been easier on her if it had happened when she was a child. Hearing details about her parents' divorce as an adult actually led her to question her own marriage.[5]

When you recall that research shows blended families have the potential for transforming children's view of marriage even after divorce, you can take heart that you may actually have made the best possible decision for shaping your children's future stability and view of marriage. And you also honored your own needs to find a close, loving partnership.

A good marriage with children is ultimately not just about the man and the woman —it transcends the couple and becomes a human laboratory for how to handle many different relationships on many levels. What your children observe about your relationship will have a great influence on how they handle future relationships with a partner, with friends, with coworkers. If they see you treating each other with care and respect, that is what they will consider normal. John's work experience as leader of a non-profit organization proved to him every day that lack of relationship skills was the key component of staff conflict. He very rarely encountered situations where lack of job skills was the issue; it was all about emotional intelligence translated into how people handle relationships. A child's relationship experiences gained through family life have a powerful influence on how well they function in their adult lives.

Work on yourself. Work on your marriage. It will amaze you what fine people your children become because you honored yourself and your partner. Significantly, through your own modeling, you will teach them how to be better partners when *they* eventually get married.

3. Boosting your self-esteem

If you're familiar with studies of human behavior, you will know that self-esteem is a major human need once your basic needs of survival are met. Self-esteem is an incredibly complex topic, and depending on whose work you read, has numerous aspects to it. First and foremost, self-esteem is an internally-generated process about your own sense of self-worth and efficacy. It's about a lot more than positive self-affirmations or being in a good relationship. In fact, if your sense of self-esteem is dependent upon the positive regard of your life partner, or in having a life partner at all, you will be on tenuous ground. One of the central lessons of both our lives is without a strong sense of self-worth, relationships can flounder.

Having said that, it is also true that positive personal relationships can help us rediscover ourselves, face up to and appreciate who we are, and learn to genuinely love ourselves. True, any relationship you're involved in is by its nature an external source of verification, but it's equally true that we fundamentally experience ourselves in relationship with others. We view a strong marital relationship not as a source of self-esteem in and of itself, but as a catalyst to help move your forward in forging an even stronger sense of self.

To have someone who loves you above all others, whose heart races at the thought of seeing you (even if you have been married for years), whose day is not complete if you're not in it, is one of the most satisfying and sought-after experiences of the human condition. Don't we all want to feel that we are the center of at least one person's universe? (Kids don't count —you are only the center of their universe for a brief amount of time. If you're not convinced, go back and re-read item one above, *Your children's job is to grow up and leave you.*) Today, the dating and matchmaking industry earns billions of dollars in the United States and Canada. To us, that's concrete proof that people want to love and be loved and that they want to find a special someone to spend their lives with. In a recent newscast we heard, there was a story about a New York man who donated sixty percent of his liver to save his wife's life. The surgery was successful. Talk about being the center of someone's universe!

Long before you were a parent, you were a young man or young woman with your own goals, needs, aspirations, and dreams. You weren't Kate's mom or Tim's dad —you were simply you. It always struck Shona as ironically symbolic that, once her son was born and particularly when he started school, she immediately ceased to be Shona but thereafter had no personal identity beyond "Ryan's mom." This feeling came not only from society but from within herself. Because this vision of parent as central role of your life is so pervasive, one of the greatest challenges you will have as a parent is helping your children develop an impression of you as a thinking, feeling, individual person in your own right. (If you're lucky, this happens when your kids are around thirty!)

In fact, Shona remembers that one of the toughest things about being a first-time stay-at-home parent was feeling a complete loss of identity. No longer was she Shona the supervisor, or Shona the speaker, or Shona the writer, or Shona who loved to travel so much. All of a sudden, she felt her life was defined by being someone's wife and someone's mother and Shona disappeared in all of that (at least for a while). It was a long and difficult struggle to rediscover who she was, one that played a huge role in the ending of her second marriage.

This loss of identify when one becomes a parent is much more common for women than for men seeing as they have traditionally (and are still largely) the parent who stays at home for a time with babies and young children. While more and more fathers are electing to stay at home with their babies (John did), and still more are becoming much more active parents than the previous generation, women are still more prone to being identified or identifying themselves as a parent first once they have children.

Men are not immune from their own identity issues, however, once they become fathers. A feeling of having much graver responsibility to be an excellent provider is a sentiment expressed by many new fathers, along with a feeling that they and they alone must carry the burden of being responsible for the physical and material needs of their family. John always says he has loved being a father, but the stress of feeling everything was on his shoulders, of often having to be the disciplinarian with his three older children, was tough to take at times. He felt a distinct loss of being able to be nurturing to his three older children because he had to be the bad guy all the time. It made him doubt his ability to be gentle and loving.

The reality is that in today's society both women and men have many challenges. Life is a struggle sometimes, no matter what your role. Our marital relationship is one of the few places where we can hope to gain some sense of ourselves as an imminently loveable, sexy, smart individual in our own right, even if we do have baby spit-up stains on our blouse and our T-shirts are fitting snugly around the beer belly we're now sporting. Your marriage is about the two of you and the two of you alone. It has nothing to do with each other's children, the children you produce together, your parents, your friends, your job, etc. It is about two people who love each other, who have made a commitment to each other, who prefer the company of each other above all other people.

Men want this kind of relationship with someone just as much as women do. Many men John has spoken to have described the empty feeling of being the logistics person —the wallet, the protector, having to be responsible for all the loud noises in the house all the time. They, too, want to be adored, appreciated for the individuals they are, loved, nurtured, and looked after. While men and women may express that need differently, it is nonetheless a driving force in human existence.

Your primary love relationship can also be a place to grow your sense of efficacy in relationships, particularly if you have been divorced. In Shona's case, after two divorces she was feeling a little beaten down in her ability to have a successful relationship. The fact that relatives kept repeating, "You're a smart woman but you're not that great at relationships," added to her self-view of being bad at relationships. She asserts that it is her relationship with John that has been a major catalyst in reversing that view of herself. When Shona expressed her fear that she was not good at relationships, John told her she'd actually done well by getting out of relationships with people who weren't willing to be the partners she needed. As time went on, and our relationship grew and strengthened, John reminded Shona from time to time that our relationship is great —so she is obviously good at it. Our partner can bring us a valuable and positive perspective about ourselves that we have failed to see.

For John, he needed to find someone who was willing to look beyond the traditional male role and see relationships as a two-way street. John no longer feels like he has to be the perfect husband and father all the time —he has some room for error and won't be smacked emotionally if he makes a mistake. All in all, he says he feels more competent, sexier, more appreciated for who he is as a person —and that he feels great to have his own personal cheering section in Shona.

As we have grown older, we have discovered the same truth every aging person knows: that each of us is secretly still eighteen years old inside, imagining ourselves with a youthful body, glowing skin, and broad sex appeal to others, even if the outer wrapper has grown considerably more worn. To go out into the world alone every day knowing there is someone who thinks you're It no matter how your appearance may change is a confidence and morale booster that will propel you to take on new challenges and learn and grow beyond what you imagined was possible. It's quite true that people are looking for that one special partner; otherwise they wouldn't keep trying again and again in relationships and marriage. Just ask Elizabeth Taylor.

Can a positive partnership alone ensure high self-esteem? Of course not. Again, it's only one of many supports that allow you to frame and reframe who you are and your own opinion of yourself. It's not about depending on your relationship for your sense of self-worth. It's about knowing that your own journey will be so much nicer when there is someone who will unfailingly be your champion, even when you make mistakes. Notice that we didn't say easier, we only said nicer. Each of us is responsible for and must struggle with our own demons whether in a relationship or not. Life is a tough enough struggle as it is. Having a positive, supportive partner is just one more way to ease that load and allow us to develop ourselves. Why wouldn't you want to build that kind of relationship?

4. Your own safe haven

Related to developing self-esteem is the idea that having a central relationship in your life is akin to having a safe haven where you can truly let your hair down —be your authentic self with no need to impress or play any role (husband, boss, mother) other than yourself.

No matter how much you love your kids, there will be times when they drive you crazy, hurt your feelings, and, yes, when you will love them but not like them very much. You don't want to announce your parenting challenges to the world, how badly you have handled some of them, how much you just want to run away today. You don't want to be alone and have no one to bounce ideas off, get feedback on actions you're considering taking, and sympathize when your big project at the office just went sideways despite your best efforts.

Nearly everyone we've talked to who is single and has become remarkably wealthy or successful in some other way comments that it's all empty when there's no one to share it with. We all need someone to celebrate with, and while your kids can be happy that you're happy, there are many things they won't or can't understand about progress you've made in your life. Only your partner, as another adult who has your best interests at heart, can do that.

When Shona's son Ryan was ten and just heading into puberty, he once commented that he didn't understand why girls wore so much makeup. "After all," he observed, "aren't you going to have to be yourself eventually? I mean, if you get married, aren't you going to have to wake up in the morning with bad breath, your hair all messy, and no makeup?" Wise words from someone not yet in his teens. He was one hundred percent right, of course. Sooner or later you have to be you, and there's no safer place to do that than with the one person who thinks you're the grandest person he or she has ever met. Everyone needs a psychological safe haven; your marriage can and should be it.

One of the ways to maintain that safe haven is to remain an interesting and stimulating person. Aside from individual self-esteem —which having your own life and interests apart from your children will surely enhance —we believe everyone has the responsibility to be the kind of person the other person wants to be with. This doesn't mean you sacrifice yourself to everything the other person wants and needs; rather, it means that you develop an active and interesting life so that you and your partner will have many things to talk about and be involved in once the main sources of your conversation and many activities (your children) have left home. This doesn't mean you have to have a supercharged career to be interesting and interested. Career is not the be-all and end-all. Many people focus their energies on other interests besides their jobs, and lifelong stay-at-home parents develop rich and diverse hobbies and interests. The key is to remain a vibrant and interesting person no matter what you do with your time.

Another way to maintain a safe haven is to continue to be loveable to the other person. Ovid once said, "If you want to be loved, be loveable."[6] This means that you continue to be kind and respectful to each other long after the first date is a very distant memory. Taking each other for granted is a common affliction in couples who have been together for a while, and particularly for couples who are parents. What continuing to be loveable looks like to us is really a collection of small things that make you want to rush home to be with each other. On cold winter nights, for example, John will go to bed before Shona and lie on her side of the bed to warm it up so she can get into a warm bed. (She has a pathological hatred of being cold!) For this small service alone, Shona has decided that John is a keeper! On days when John has clearly had enough of children, Shona will send him to his room with a good book and instructions to just relax and leave the kids up to her that night. He brings her flowers for no reason, she hands him his towel when he gets out of the shower. He buys her the rare candy she remembers from her childhood, she finds his favorite pastries even though they're no good for him. He cooks her favorite meals, she makes sure his shirts are ironed and hung up in the closet.

Events come and go, but your love for each other is constant. When life seems out of control, frustrating, stressful, and you feel like you are at your wit's end, go to your spouse and say, "I love you. I chose to spend my life with you." We guarantee it will give you some perspective on your troubles and remind you of the safe haven you have in your partner.

Chapter Four

Time, Space, and Black Holes

To live is so startling, it leaves little time for anything else.[1]
- Emily Dickinson

There is one universal element that unites all couples in a family, whether intact or blended: not enough time and, frequently, not enough space. We mentioned in the last chapter that it is important for the two of you to have time together away from the kids. It's also important that you have space that's specifically yours as well. One of the things we have discovered through trial and error (three marriages between us plus our own), is that time and space are extremely important elements for any couple. In the absence of setting aside that time and space, your relationship can get sucked into a "black hole," never to be seen again.

Establishing and maintaining connection

Here's what we mean. A black hole is a collapsed star in space, a region in which everything is absorbed and from which nothing can escape, not even light. It has been our experience in marriages and relationships that without adequate time and attention paid to each other, that's exactly what happens to your relationship —it gets sucked into some kind of black hole where the connection you once had disappears, and you are left with the sensation that you are roommates with little or nothing in common.

We are not talking about common interests here. Many couples can and do have very different interests from each other. Rather, we are talking about something we believe is of a higher order than common interests —a sense of connection to each other.

We discovered this tendency to lose connection quite early in our blended family life, but it took us a while to be able to articulate it. It started out as a vague sense of separateness or disconnection with each other brought on by our busy work and home lives. We found that if we went any longer than a week without having some connection time with each other (time and/or space away from work, activities, and the children), we would begin to feel cut off from our emotional closeness. We believe we have an extremely strong and close relationship; our relationship is the number one priority in both of our lives. That's why we found it so scary to realize that all it took was about a week for that sense of closeness to get eroded by the sheer volume of the demands of life.

Upon reflection, we realized that we had allowed this sense of separateness to flourish with our former spouses, finally culminating in the end of our marriages when we couldn't really remember what it was that had brought us together in the first place. As we said earlier, this can go on for years because the kids serve as a convenient and consuming distraction for however many years they are at home and you are raising them. Sooner or later, however, it will be back to the two of you.

So what exactly do we mean by a sense of connection? It is commonly repeated that marriage takes work —unceasing effort to ensure your partner is happy and that your relationship is on solid ground. It can mean many different things to many different people, but generally speaking, we believe it means paying attention to your relationship. To us, work sounds a little negative, implying huge amounts of energy and effort. We don't know about you, but we find that an extremely unappealing way to describe our number one relationship in life. Personally, we don't find that our relationship takes huge amounts of energy and effort —it feels nice, comfortable, and what we *want* to do, not what we *have* to do.

The most important part of this concept of connection for us is that we do not let more than a couple of days go by without articulating something we have noticed about the other person, our way of communicating, whatever. For example, if John notices that Shona has been fairly quiet for a couple of evenings, he will ask her if she's worried about something, if something is bothering her, or if there's something she wants to talk about. This may sound relatively minor, but as time goes by, relatively minor things pile up and eat away at your relationship. What Shona is being quiet about may have little or nothing to do with the relationship, but the fact that John has noticed something is going on provides a sense of connection.

Sometimes, what's bothering Shona *is* about the relationship, in which case John's inquiry provides a great opportunity to uncover it. The reality is that in many relationships numerous issues go unresolved because people don't voice them. Sometimes Shona will voice them herself, sometimes it takes John's inquiry to bring them out. It doesn't much matter how it occurs as long as it does occur. If you have the slightest sense that something is going on with your spouse and can't put your finger on it, ask. And if they say "nothing," don't stop. Many of us have been trained to say "nothing" because we don't want to bother others or we believe the other person might think what troubles us is stupid.

Many women reading this may well be thinking at this point that it's okay to say all of this about noticing and talking, but most men will not do it. It's true that most men will not naturally engage in relationship discussions on a regular basis, but it's also true that just checking in with them from time to time shows them you care. Ladies, this is not the time to get all self-righteous about how you are the one who always has to ask and do the talking. It doesn't matter who initiates it as long as it gets done. Women and men do have vastly different styles of communication but neither is wrong, they're just different. When you understand that men are trained to keep their innermost thoughts and feelings to themselves, it may help you to not misinterpret their silence as disinterest. On the upside, a man typically considers his wife his best friend; she is often the only person in his life he will talk to about anything personal. Having said all that, we know it's a lot easier said than done. This is one of those moments when we're asking you to bear with us for now. We *will* address the fundamental differences in male/female communication in the Communication section of this book.

Significantly, Dr. Bray found in his studies of stepfamilies that conflict and turmoil in the relationship and family often surfaced much more regularly —received attention —than in intact families. "The presence of children requires near-total personal disclosure, and near-total personal disclosure promotes an unusual degree of emotional closeness."[2] Ironically, being less willing to tolerate conflict and turmoil and more willing to make an effort to do small things can help people be better communicators and may well give the next marriage/relationship a better chance at survival.

Another element of connection is just plain spending time together. If you notice that several days in a row go by and you haven't had one moment alone to reconnect with each other, say so. And then agree on a time that the two of you will be together within the next couple of days. It could be as simple as a twenty-minute walk around the block or down to the corner store with the dog. That's plenty of time to chat, hold hands, and just unwind *together* from your hectic day. We can't emphasize this enough. The longer the two of you are apart, either physically or mentally, the easier it will become to continue that separateness. The more you feel separate, the more you will not want to reengage with the person. And the more you don't engage, the more you will forget how and why you even wanted to in the first place.

Connection isn't just about talking and time, though. It can be established in numerous little ways: You notice when your spouse is looking stressed and overworked, and you keep the kids away from him or her that night so he or she can have some solitude to regroup. You buy something with the groceries or when you're getting gas that you know your spouse likes (even if you don't) — it doesn't have to be big, just a small something that says you were thinking about him or her (a chocolate, a rose, a book, a fridge magnet). You arrange for a babysitter so the two of you can have a date (more on this later) and surprise your spouse. You pick up the kids from the sitter even though your spouse is always the one who gets them on his or her way home from work. You cook dinner even though that's not usually your job. You take your wife to a chick flick without complaining; you go to an action movie with your husband without complaining. You phone him or her at work for no particular reason just to say "I love you." Some people put these things in the category of work; again, we call it paying attention. The main difference between work and paying attention is "have to" versus "want to." You make dinner for your spouse one night to keep him or her happy because you want to, not because you have to. There's a huge difference in our mind.

There is an old saying, "Find a job you love and you'll never work a day in your life." We feel that way about relationships too. "Find a partner you love, and you'll never have to work at it." To us, relationships aren't about hard, slogging effort but rather about keeping that person primary in your life and continuing to connect with him or her.

One man we know who was facilitating a training session for thirty-five salesmen asked them about the last time, aside from Christmas, their anniversary, and her birthday, any of them had surprised his wife with a special gift. Of the thirty-five, only one had done something in the past month. Many said it had been somewhere between three and six months. Over a third couldn't remember. His point? Relationships need planned attention. If you value your marital relationship above all others, it isn't work — it's play. Everybody feels good.

An important part of connection for us is intimacy. If our days have been too hectic with work and home/child-centered activities, sex is often a way to find reconnection both emotionally and physically. It creates an intimacy —and reestablishes it —which we have found is far more important than the physical experience itself. It is easy to feel too tired at the end of the day to make love. If that's the case with you, then find another time. Occasionally, John will call Shona at work to see if she can leave a little early that day and meet him at home before the kids get there. It's even better if he makes the call before noon because then both of us are thinking about our tryst all day at work. It gives us something to look forward to and puts us in the frame of mind to really connect with each other —and not just on a physical level.

If getting off work early is not practical for you, plan to wake up fifteen minutes earlier one morning (yes, you can actually give up your workout for one day without it undoing any of your hard work). Believe it or not, planning a sexual encounter can be exciting. If none of that is workable for you, send the kids out to a park for half an hour, or to a friend's, or whatever during the afternoon. Take that opportunity to reconnect physically. And make sure that you initiate sex once in while, especially if you're the one who usually doesn't. This is a very important source of connection for your spouse, who will be delighted that you are showing interest.

We think this loss of connection is what happens to a lot of couples' sex lives. It's quite a common theme in the media to have married partners complain that a wife or husband never wants to have sex anymore. Worse, it's portrayed as a reward for something. (There's that transactional thing again: I did something nice, now you owe me sex.) Worse still, it's withheld as a punishment.

It is very dangerous to view sex from a transactional point of view. Ultimately, it degrades your relationship; sex without mutual desire is duty, and that is symptomatic of larger issues. If you're both accountable and responsible for paying attention to the relationship, your sexual relationship is no different than some of the other things we have mentioned that create connection.

Sex between two people who love each other is a prime source of connection, and something that should be attended to on a fairly regular basis or you will lose a physical as well as an emotional sense of connection. When you haven't connected physically for a while, it becomes difficult to ask for sex because then you appear needy. This all becomes a vicious circle of lack of connection, leading to lack of intimacy, which leads to even more lack of connection.

Statistics show that most people have sex about 2.6 times a week[3] (we're not sure what the .6 means, but okay). It seems our busy lives don't allow for more, especially when we have all kinds of children around. Only the two of you can decide what is a right amount for both of you, but we stress that quality is more important than quantity. The goal is to keep emotionally connected with one another, not to win some kind of sexual marathon.

Later on, when we talk about the notion of Acceptance in the Recipe for Blended Family Success®, you will see why connection becomes so critical. You can put up with a lot as long as your intimacy and connection needs are taken care of. Without connection with your partner, you're living your life alone in a more complex and stressful situation (the blended family) than you would be if you really *were* living alone. And one of the worst feelings in the world is to feel alone when you're surrounded by people.

Protected time

While we've talked about day-to-day practices for maintaining connection, there is something else you must attend to so that your relationship stays on solid ground: establishing protected time for the two of you. These are *regular* blocks of time everyone in the family knows are just for the two of you and which do not involve children. Our experience and best recommendation for protected time is to establish a regular date night. It doesn't have to be every week, but should be regular enough that the children get used to it and accept it as normal.

Our date nights are generally a Saturday night once a month where it's just the two of us —no children, no friends, no other family members. We often just go out for a long, leisurely dinner. Sometimes we go to a movie too, but generally we find movies aren't great for connection because we aren't talking to one another. Many times after dinner we'll go for a walk and browse around some stores we like. Often, we will spend time at the local bookstore where we enjoy an after-dinner coffee and look at travel books about places we want to go or just browse through books we have similar interests in. Sometimes, we just sit and talk more. It doesn't much matter what you do or what your interests are, just as long as you do it on a recurring basis.

It is an interesting thing about parents and stepparents that while they often feel the need to have some time away from their children, as soon as they do, all they talk about is the children! That's certainly where we go first, too, and we often find the beginning of our date conversations to be about the children, their activities, any concerns, etc. But we allow only a certain amount of conversation about the children (about half an hour), and the rest of the evening has to be about something else. Is one of us dreaming about taking a new course? How long will it take us to save for a trip to Spain? How can John achieve his goal of getting more exercise? What new recipe has he found that he's dying to try? What plan is Shona hatching for her next writing project? How is she feeling about turning forty? Generally, we talk about stuff that is near, dear, and personal to our hearts as individuals and as a couple, because we spend so much of our other time dealing with and talking about the children. This is our one chance to hope and dream as individuals and as a couple with our own separate, adult interests.

Whatever you choose for your date night, be sure to pick a time that works for you. We mostly go out on Saturdays because we find on Friday nights we are both too worn out from the week to be able to relax and really enjoy one another. Friday is also often a family-oriented night when we watch movies or play games with the children and generally unwind together. Likewise, daytime hours during the weekends are often taken up with family-oriented chores and activities (taking the kids to activities/birthday parties, doing yard work, cleaning the house, etc.). Maybe Wednesdays are better for you. It doesn't much matter —just pick a regular time that you will adhere to at least once a month. In the last chapter, we indicated that one key reason to put your marriage first is so that you can have a safe haven from the world. Having a date night is a key facilitator of that safe haven feeling. It allows you to disengage *together* from the worries and stresses of the world.

Date nights are not the only protected time we have established for ourselves; however, they *are* the largest and most consistent blocks of time. There are three other times that are generally known to our children to be for us alone. The first time is between six-thirty and six-forty-five a.m. We like to sit in our living room and have coffee together to start our day. The children are usually still asleep, and we find it a relaxing way to start what are usually very hectic days for both of us.

The second time is after dinner, also often having coffee. John makes dinner while Shona works out and picks up Kate from daycare, having it all ready for their arrival. Dinner is mostly family time; we all talk about our day and the children review any homework or other activities they have that night. Because we are right into family time as soon as Shona gets home, we find having an after-dinner coffee together while the children are doing chores or homework is also a nice time to connect and unwind together from the day.

The last time is after nine p.m. This is when the children are in bed and we have finished whatever activities we needed to do with them or individually. We find this time period to be the toughest one to navigate, however. If one of us is out for the evening, it obviously doesn't happen. One of us might be really tired and already asleep, or one person might be working on an individual project or reading a book. We also found this a more difficult time when we had older children in the house. Older children are naturally up and about (and therefore more noisy and distracting) much later than younger children, and it was particularly difficult to find evening time together in that situation. In fact, one of the most challenging times for us as a couple was when we had older *and* very young children in the house at the same time —the older children would often be around until midnight, and the baby was up through the night and the early hours of the morning. We rarely had any peace and quiet, never mind time alone in the evening during those days.

While these three connection times don't always work out, we do try to grab them whenever we can. When we find those times are getting interrupted too much, we reiterate to the children that those times are ours, but they are less written in stone due to day-to-day challenges such as early or late meetings, children's activities, sick children, etc.

Protected space

Not too long ago, it was very common for most North American children to grow up sharing a bedroom. These days, it's much more common for children to grow up never sharing a bedroom. We believe it is very important in blended families for each child as well as the couple to have protected space —a place where they can go to be alone and have their own stuff. If you can't swing having a separate bedroom for each child, set up shared bedroom spaces with provisions for shutting out the world, such as putting up a curtain between each child's part of the bedroom that can be opened or closed when needed, or placing a large bookcase (or two bookcases back to back) in the middle of the room to at least provide some demarcation of individual space.

Protected space is equally important for the couple in a blended family. Unless you are lucky enough to be able to afford a very large home with many bedrooms and plenty of common space for the whole family, you are likely going to find that merging your two families makes your home a lot more hectic than it used to be. In that case, it is extremely important that you as a couple have a space that is just yours. Often, this means the bedroom. Our bedroom is the scene of many quiet conversations after dinner or simply just a peaceful oasis in the course of a hectic week. Our children have all been taught that this is not a room they can barge into at any time. Even as young as four, Kate was taught the same thing. Everyone is required to knock before entering and to wait to be invited in before proceeding.

While we have a television in our bedroom, it is not very often that the children are allowed to watch it when another child is watching a different show in the family room. The reason for this is simple — the rest of space in the house is what we refer to as common space (except the kids' bedrooms), where everyone is free to roam, come and go, and generally make use of. In our modest home, this means it is rare to be in one room alone without someone else being there or at least nearby engaged in some sort of activity. Our bedroom is basically the only space that is ours and ours alone. In the same way that children are protective of and need their own space, so do adults. We believe many parents make the mistake of thinking children's space is children's space, and parents' space is everyone's space. We consider our bedroom a place of connection with each other, and not just in the sexual sense. As a blended family couple, you have probably never had the luxury of living alone together in a home with no children, so your bedroom becomes an even more important place to solidify your relationship and connection.

Other than when seven-year-old Kate was a baby and when either of the young children have occasional nightmares, no one sleeps in our bed with us. It is important in a blended family to maintain this kind of sanctity for your bedroom, for it's one of the few things that is truly yours together. Doing otherwise means you run the risk of feeling your relationship is being imposed upon (it is), which can easily lead to a loss of connection because you are forced to deal with constant interruptions in your protected space. After a while, it's not protected anymore, and you will have lost an important tool to maintain the strength of your couple relationship.

Before we got together, it was Ryan's habit to get into bed with Shona on weekend mornings. After we got together, we mostly weaned him off this habit (he was five at the time).

There were several reasons for this. First, it was symbolic that the space was now ours as a couple, and not Mom and Ryan's. That didn't mean that Ryan didn't get alone or snugly time with Shona —it just meant that he couldn't expect to do it every weekend. Shona then developed a habit of lying in Ryan's bed at night when tucking him in, either to read a story or just to talk. This satisfied Ryan's need for some cozy connection with his mom, but also protected our private space as a couple.

Protecting this space was a bigger issue at the outset for John than it was for Shona because John's family moved into Shona's house. John and his daughter, Rudie, needed to feel like the house and the bedroom were equally their territory and we needed to make it clear to all the children, particularly those who already lived in the house, that John and Rudie had a right to be there and have their personal space needs respected. We recommend that, whenever possible, you move into a completely new house where no one has territory issues. However, we realize it isn't always practical or affordable to do that (it certainly wasn't for us), and that's when setting boundaries around space becomes doubly important.

A final note on the space that will be your sanctuary as a couple. If either one of you is at all introverted, be aware that it will be tempting to use that protected space as a frequent escape —and too much can be unhealthy. In our relationship, John is much more of an introvert than Shona; therefore being around people gets exhausting and stressful much more quickly for him. When he is going through particularly stressful times, he can develop a tendency to retreat to the bedroom too much. That's where the noticing and talking strategy kicks in again. On several occasions, Shona has had to point out to John that the sanctuary is becoming more of a retreat, and that he needs to reengage with her and with the family.

❧

We don't feel we can leave the issues of protected time and space without adding one last reason for their importance: the simple fact that you are dealing with a lot more people in your life. And it's not just your immediate blended family —it's all of their relatives, other half siblings, ex-spouses, new partners, etc. Sometimes, whether you choose to or not, it can feel like you are playing host to a cast of thousands. We remember one memorable Christmas where Shona's ex-husband and current girlfriend and John's ex-wife, along with all the children, assembled in our living room for drinks and gift opening. Another time involved one child's high school graduation where there was coming and going all day by various and sundry family members who had a connection to the graduating child —and most were not related to each other. That day, the house felt like Grand Central Station. In situations like these, it becomes even more important for you to find a place and time to escape, regroup, and recharge.

Not being able to do that for several months had a very stressful effect on Shona one fall. So many people had been living in and visiting the house that she felt her sanctuary had been taken over. Never one for crying much, she found herself crying in frustration over two relatively minor incidents with various children over the course of one week. Because it was uncharacteristic for her, both of us knew it was time for a break. So she took herself off to a hotel room for a weekend in the nearest city and just revelled in the peace and quiet, as well as the lack of responsibility. She read books, watched movies, and basically did nothing —by herself. The downside to this is, of course, the other partner is left holding the bag for everything at home in addition to the fact that you're away from each other. Not only that, we both knew it wasn't right when the only way you feel you can recharge is to find time and space away from the place that is supposed to be your sanctuary. That runaway weekend taught us a lot about how we needed to set boundaries and create house rules to keep our sanity intact. Reviewing our family vision, described in the next chapter, helped with that, in addition to other tools we'll describe later.

Chapter Five

Creating Your Family Vision

Many marriages would be better if the husband and the wife clearly understood that they are on the same side.[1]
Zig Ziglar

One of your primary responsibilities as a couple within a blended family is creating a joint vision for what your family will be and do. Remember how we mentioned that you and your partner are the Change Transition Team for your family? Well, all change managers start with one key concept in bringing about effective and lasting change: they start with a clear and compelling vision they can share with and use to guide people through the rocky roads ahead. That is your first task as the Change Transition Team: creating a family vision. We don't mean it has to be written down and posted on a bulletin board like a corporate vision statement. We do mean that the two of you have to talk about how you see the family functioning on a basic level. Our experience has taught us that the foundation of a family vision is being willing to go outside the lines of what has been normal for you.

Going outside the lines

One thing is certain: your vision for your family will be as unique and individual as your family is. There has never been a one-size-fits-all vision for a nuclear family, and there certainly isn't one for a blended family either. Beware, though, you might experience some resistance from members of your extended family and society as a whole when you create your family in a way that suits you.

For example, when we discovered that Shona was pregnant, we made a decision that she would take only a short time off work and John would be a stay-at-home parent for a year. There were some personal as well as practical reasons for this decision. First, John had given up a job to blend his family with Shona's in a distant city and was unemployed. Even when he was employed, Shona earned a higher salary than he did. Additionally, John had been a special needs teacher up to that point, but he didn't want to continue doing that and because he wasn't sure where he wanted to go next in his career he wanted some time to think about it. Shona had a job she loved to go back to at a salary that would easily maintain the family.

As we already discussed, Shona knew from the experience of having her first child that she wasn't the kind of mother who thrived on staying at home with her baby for long periods of time. For his part, John welcomed the opportunity to stay home with the baby as he had missed that opportunity with his three older children because he had been so busy working. It was a decision that both of us were happy with for a variety of personal and professional reasons.

This decision turned out to be a wonderful one for our daughter Kate as well. For the first three months of her life, Shona was her primary caregiver, but John was also actively involved as he was home fulltime as well. This developed a strong bond between Shona and Kate, but it also allowed John to develop a firm connection. Once Shona returned to work, John became the primary caregiver and developed an even closer bond with Kate. When he eventually began a new job just after Kate turned one, he felt secure and happy that he had given his daughter a strong start. To this day, Kate maintains a very close and strong bond with both of us, and will go to each of us equally for comfort and attention.

Kate loves to paint her finger and toe nails pretty colors. Being so young, she is rarely able to accomplish this without going outside the lines. Blended families are like that too — to create a vision that works for everyone, you have to be willing to go outside the lines and question the way things have always been done or "the right way." As we mentioned earlier, many people living in blended families have no idea what the rules are because they grew up in intact, nuclear families just as John and I did. Even if you did grow up in a blended family, every family is unique and presents different challenges. Both of us are the first to admit that we didn't know what to do on many occasions, and while our parents are well-meaning and wise in their own way, none of them could really give us any practical advice other than generalities because they simply had no experience navigating the challenges of blended family life.

Which is probably why our parents were somewhat bothered by the fact that John was a stay-at-home dad for a year. Both sets struggled with their generation's notion that the man is the provider, and seeing as we had completely turned that notion upside down, were confused about the situation.

This acceptance of father as primary caregiver is also still not well accepted in society as a whole, even though we like to think we've come a long way in that regard. John would often put Kate in her stroller during the day and take her to a local park where he would encounter stay-at-home moms with their toddlers looking askance at his presence. A number of the women assumed he was divorced and with his daughter for visitation times. Others asked if he was babysitting while Mom was at an appointment. He often felt like an intruder and even felt that certain women looked at him suspiciously.

Another thing our parents were uncomfortable with was the fact Shona didn't change her name when she married John. Shona's parents continually and vocally struggled with how to address mail to both of us ("It just doesn't feel right to write 'Shona Welsh and John Penton.'"), for example, while John's parents lamented the fact that because we didn't get married before Kate was born, she would not have her dad's last name.

Again, they were caught in traditional thinking that dictated women changed their names when they got married, and that children born 'out of wedlock' (what an incredibly unfortunate term) could not claim the father's name. For the record, Kate was given a hyphenated last name at birth that combines both of our names.

Shona experienced equal commentary at her job, where ninety-five percent of her colleagues were men. When they asked what John did for a living and she explained he was a stay-at-home dad, conversation would stop and the men would get funny looks on their faces. In a technical field populated mostly by men, stay-at-home dads were completely out of their realm of experience. The management of the company (largely over forty) also struggled with Shona not changing her name, continually asking Shona after we got married when she was issuing an e-mail with her new name.

On one notable occasion, Shona was speaking at a formal dinner. When the MC got up to introduce her, one of his comments was, "I don't know why her name is different than her husband's — that's kind of strange, but there you go."

Those were the easy issues because in the first instance — Shona's name — it was a decision discussed and agreed on between the two of us. In the second instance — the naming and care of Kate — she was our child together, so we had no previous family culture or non-custodial parent issues to deal with before coming to a decision.

The tough part of creating a vision for your blended family comes with the "yours and mine" part of the equation: family rules/behavior, family traditions, conflict resolution styles, relationships with ex-spouses, you name it. In our case the situation looked like this: John was moving into Shona's house, which she had been sharing with her five-year-old son Ryan, with his fifteen-year-old daughter Rudie. His son Tim, then seventeen, was living with his mother, and his son Paul-Andrew, nineteen, had effectively left home. However, just because your stepchildren are grown up doesn't mean they don't have a role to play and that they won't have an effect on your blended family situation. They most certainly do and we'll get into that in more detail later. Also, in the age of boomerang children —where grown children return home after having left one or several times —you need to be prepared for your blended family to form and reform numerous times.

Rudie was *not* happy about being taken away from all of her friends and her old school. She was also going to be a nine-hour drive away from her mother, which she accepted, but it bothered her. Ryan was not happy about having to share his mom with these other people, not to mention that he could no longer have the run of the house. He didn't know what having a step dad meant —didn't he already have a dad? Adding insult to injury for him, he had to give up his room across from Mom's so the baby could have it when she was born. He also had to give up dibs on the biggest bedroom available so Rudie could have it. He still, however, had a bedroom of his own that we hurriedly built before Kate was born.

On the plus side, all the kids were excited about the baby. The older kids were unfailingly kind to Ryan, apart from the odd time when he drove them crazy (which is quite normal), and Ryan liked the older kids, all of whom he continues to look up to even now. Rudie and Shona liked each other and got along well, and Ryan saw that John made his mom very happy so he was willing to give him a chance.

So, it's pretty clear you need to be prepared to go in your own direction when it comes to creating a vision for your blended family. After you've decided which lines you're going to go outside of that work for you, there are three more key issues you must attend to immediately if your blended family is to get off to a good start: family rules and behavior, parenting and discipline, and family traditions.

Family rules and behavior

In all the books and research we have read on blended families, one common theme that emerges is that of family meetings. While we hadn't read any of those books when we first got together, we're pleased to say that a family meeting is indeed one of the first things we did.

Our first family meeting took place in the living room with us, Rudie, and Ryan. While Tim and Paul-Andrew were not initially part of this, they got involved in modified ways later on when Tim moved in for months at a time and Paul-Andrew came to live for short periods between jobs. Because there was such an age difference between Rudie and Ryan (she was fifteen, Ryan was five), we felt it was important to clearly define the general house rules, as well as what were teenage- versus young-child-specific rules.

For example, one thing we made clear up front with Rudie was that she was not going to become the babysitter for either Ryan or the new baby. While it was not unreasonable to expect that she would look after the children from time to time (as is the case in all families), we wanted to ensure that she knew we did not want to abuse her good will or her time. Having an instant younger brother and sister was, after all, not her choice, although she accepted it with cheerfulness and a willingness to help. We always honored that agreement, and insisted that if she ever felt we were abusing it she needed to say so. It never came up, although we would check with her every once in while to ensure she was feeling okay about it. When we asked her to baby sit, we always made it clear it was her choice and that she would be paid, just like we would pay another babysitter (this applied to long periods of time, not quick trips to the store when we needed her to watch the kids for a few minutes). She always appreciated that, and we think it went a long way toward maintaining good will in our blended family. In fact, this arrangement was made clear to all three of the older children, which in the end resulted in a genuine willingness and frequent offers on their part to baby sit so we could get away for an evening.

Other examples of teenage-specific rules included what chores we expected Rudie to do, what time at night we expected all phone calls to cease, how loud her music could be and when, standards of cleanliness for her room, car usage, etc. You will never think of everything, but as much as you can get on the table up front will serve you well when situations arise and you've got an agreement in place to deal with them.

Ryan was also told about chores, which was something new for him as, up to that point, we had a live-in nanny who had done most of the work. It had been appropriate up to that point, but he was about to turn six and the family had swelled to more than twice its size, so he had to learn how to contribute as part of keeping a family going. He was assigned simple chores such as setting the table for meals, carrying the compost bucket out to the backyard, putting the recycling in appropriate bins, etc.

Everyone had to learn how to be considerate of the fact that the baby was sleeping and that we now kept conservative hours out of necessity. Rudie had to learn how to keep a teenager's sometimes loud, late hours within an appropriate window of acceptability, and Ryan had to learn to play quietly during Kate's nap time. Both Rudie and Ryan had to learn how to respect each other's space —at first, Ryan continually walked in on Rudie in the bathroom and her room until taught otherwise.

Shona had to learn not to freak out every time Rudie took one of the family cars (she had never had to share hard-earned and valuable things with a child before) and to break out of patterned habits of reacting to teenagers' normal tendencies for challenging rules and asserting independence.

One family trait that particularly annoyed Shona was Rudie's habit of removing Shona's wet clothes from the washing machine and dumping them on top of the dryer so she could do her own clothes. The first few times, Shona said nothing but just quietly stewed (one is anxious to keep the waters smooth in the first days of a blended family), but she finally had to address it. She explained that in her family, the rule had been that if you found someone else's wet stuff in the washer, you were to put it in the dryer and turn the dryer on before proceeding with your own laundry. Before drying your own clothes, you were to remove the other person's now-dry clothes and place them in the person's room. You didn't have to fold them —just put them on the person's bed.

To Shona's surprise, Rudie was pleasantly agreeable to this rule as she felt she would benefit from it as well. If someone found her wet stuff in the washer, she could be assured it would be dried. She explained to Shona that, after having lived with two brothers and her dad for the past four years, she was so used to just dumping stuff (housework and laundry were not her dad's or the boys' strengths) that it had just become normal to her. In truth, she said, she preferred Shona's way.

There is a whole range of small, day-to-day interactions like that one that you can't possibly anticipate when you set family rules. The trick is to surface them quickly and find a compromise all of you can live with as soon as possible.

Another incident occurred after Tim moved in with us. Ryan had been watching TV in the family room when Tim entered and wanted to do some homework on the computer. Tim told Ryan he had to turn off the TV so he could concentrate. Ryan was justifiably offended, feeling he had been in the family room first and that Tim had no right to tell him to stop what he was doing just so he could do what he wanted. In discussing the situation with Tim, it became apparent that there was no ill intent involved. He was simply not used to having to consider that a young child's interests, however irrelevant and irritating to him, needed to be respected and honored. We worked out a suitable schedule where Ryan could watch his favorite TV shows and Tim would use the computer after Ryan was in bed or doing some other activity.

Most interactions in blended families are as minor as the ones we've described, but as the old saying goes, "God is in the details." You will be able to anticipate global issues and discuss them up front, but day-to-day things like this will jump up and bite you unexpectedly, and you need to be prepared to approach each situation with rationality, a willingness to understand, and your best calm, conflict-resolution skills. Although the situation with Tim turned out fine and to everyone's satisfaction, Shona's first, emotional reaction was to be annoyed with Tim for imposing on Ryan's rights. Your first tendency will naturally be to defend your own child, but a wiser approach is to hear both parties out before you jump to conclusions. Most of the time, your stepchildren are either simply unaware of the effect of their behavior or haven't thought their decision through. This is as true of older children as it is of younger children. Remember, everyone is coping with and trying to figure out the rules of the game in this new, blended family. It is a very different game than the one they are used to. We will discuss specific family rules, including standards of conflict resolution and how we treat one another, in more detail in the section on Communication.

Parenting and discipline

Often a source of contention for new blended families, parenting styles and our different perceptions about what needed to happen caused us to struggle from the very beginning. We had both been single parents for a while before we met, had both adopted differing parenting styles, and now had to merge those styles to respond to all of the children.

With the new baby we had a lot more time to talk about things as she grew and come to some consensus about our parenting styles, what we felt was important, and how to handle certain situations. We didn't have that luxury with Rudie and Ryan. They were instantly part of our combined family and consequently we were instantly both responsible for parenting.

The approach you need to take in parenting a teenager is, of course, very different than the approach you need to take with a younger child. Parenting patterns are much more set in a child's mind by the time he or she reaches the teen years, and introducing a whole new —and completely different — parenting element at that age can be particularly challenging. One of the biggest struggles Shona had was deciding what role she should/needed to play in certain situations —and it often changed. For example, when Rudie came to her with problems she wished to discuss and wanted the opinion of another female, it was easy to play the role of trusted older friend. This was more comfortable for Shona because she found it much easier than on the occasions where she had to deal with situations that required a parent's perspective or discipline.

Whether or not John was home, Shona would be forced every day to make split-second decisions on whether she needed to be a parent or a friend to Rudie, depending on the situation. It was a very fine line to walk, and often not very clear-cut. Most of the time, she was unsure about what to do. Rudie was not a bad teenager at all and her missteps were of the usual teenage variety but there were still times that Shona had to play the uncomfortable role of disciplinarian.

One incident involved overhearing a conversation Rudie was having with a friend regarding the purchase of some marijuana. Aside from the serious legal issues, there was a personal moral issue for Shona as well, one that she had been clear about with Rudie on numerous occasions. She had been emphatic that drug use of any sort would not be tolerated in the family. Shona had a few bad moments over this situation, having to weigh a number of factors to decide the right course of action —and one that she could live with herself, including:

-her responsibility as the pseudo parent and legal guardian of Rudie

- her responsibility as a law-abiding citizen

- her desire to be a source of wiser, older female support and counsel (and being afraid to jeopardize that new and therefore tenuous relationship)

- her regret that she had overheard it in the first place (and wishing she hadn't so she wouldn't have to deal with it)

- her unwillingness to conceal anything from John (she considered not telling him at all clearly inappropriate as he was Rudie's biological father, not to mention that keeping secrets was not part of our trusting relationship).

She also had a dawning realization (here was a nice part of this challenging situation) that she had a desire to protect Rudie from harm because she genuinely cared about her. One of the great lessons of being a stepparent as well as a parent is that you can feel many conflicting emotions at the same time, some good and some bad.

In the end, Shona did the only thing she could and should do — she told John. We had a discussion regarding the best course of action with Rudie. The result was that we had a frank discussion with Rudie about the possible consequences of her actions, she was not permitted to take the car out that night, and, yes, she was mightily upset with Shona on two counts — one, that she had overhead the conversation in the first place, and two, that she had been ratted out. Shona had not been listening at Rudie's door, but she had been folding some laundry near Rudie's bedroom; with the door ajar and Rudie making no attempt to quiet her voice, it was inevitable Shona would hear her. This, like all things, passed within a few days.

Generally speaking, we believe the key to step parenting older children is to be as open and honest with them as possible — make your thinking transparent (we'll talk more on this is the Acceptance section). Shona can't think of any occasion when she had to play a parent role with Rudie when she didn't at least try to lay out the reasoning for her actions and engage in some sort of dialogue. This doesn't mean Shona was perfect all the time. Sometimes she overreacted or just plain reacted to the fact that she often felt like she was dealing with an adult roommate in the house when she had long since outgrown her roommate years. For her part, Rudie was (and still is) an incredibly fair-minded and reasonable person for her years, and could often see or understand Shona's perspective, even if she didn't like or agree with it.

There were several times — not during times of tension — when Rudie and Shona openly discussed the fact that neither would have chosen to have their lives turned upside down by having to merge into a blended family. Shona clearly understood that Rudie resented being yanked away from her boyfriend, best friends, and mother two years before finishing high school, and Rudie clearly understood that becoming an instant mother to teenagers and having to give up a great deal of her house to her new blended family was a challenge for Shona as well. It didn't mean they didn't like each other or didn't want to get along — it simply gave them a better understanding of the complexities of each other's situation.

On the upside (and there were many positive times), Shona was often in a position to defend Rudie's female interests and desires when John was at a loss or completely oblivious to Rudie's motivations. Reality is, John has never been a teenage girl so some of her behaviors and interests genuinely confounded him while they made perfect sense to Shona; there were occasions when he would react with offhand comments or only passing concern to issues that seemed huge to Rudie. Shona was often able to bridge the communication gap between the two of them and give John some perspective about Rudie's focus. In fact, sometimes John found himself feeling jealous that Rudie would go to Shona with some issues before she'd go to him, and he has an ongoing sense of guilt that all of his older children will sometimes approach Shona instead of him. On balance, though, John is very pleased that his three older children get along well with Shona. Again, the emotions that the blended family experience elicits are often complex and paradoxical.

In some ways, establishing John's role as a stepfather to Ryan was easier than Shona's experience with Rudie. There isn't as much conflict over when to be a friend and when to be a parent when the child is quite young. In other ways, it was just as challenging.

One thing Ryan made sure to do from the very beginning was to make it clear that he already had a dad. John has never failed to honor and support that, and we were very careful to gradually introduce and grow his role of stepfather (and disciplinarian). All the books we have read on this issue support this gradual assumption of disciplinary duties. Ultimately, however, we believe that when you are dealing with a child as young as six (or younger) you can and should build a role for the stepparent that is more fully parent than the parent/friend combination that characterizes a step relationship with older children.

John picked his opportunities carefully, and it was a combination of discipline opportunities and fun/bonding opportunities. The first discipline opportunity arose one day when John was building something in the garage and six-year-old Ryan, being interested in what was going on, sat down to watch and chat with John. Things were going quite well until Ryan picked up a hammer and began playing with it. John calmly asked him to put the hammer down because he was not handling it safely. Ryan just went on playing with the hammer. John calmly asked him again, and still Ryan didn't put the hammer down. Instead, he looked John straight in the eye daring him to make him do it. It was a moment of truth for both of them.

The power of John's "teacher voice," as we call it, is that it is decisive, clear, and louder than he usually speaks, considering that John is generally a fairly soft-spoken individual. "Put it down now!" John said in his best teacher voice, startling Ryan to attention —and to promptly put down the hammer. It was the beginning of establishing a clear parenting relationship between John and Ryan. In the years since then, Ryan will often comment that he doesn't wish to get in trouble because he just hates to be the focus of that teacher voice! Of course, he is quite happy when his little sister is the one under the gun.

Please don't think that John didn't have some misgivings about the incident. In fact, he went to Shona after it happened to explain what he had done and why. Even though he knew he would have to assume a disciplinarian role over time, it was still nerve-racking and he still felt he needed to check perception with Shona. After nine years, of course, we no longer feel the need to check with each other on approaches to discipline as we have a clear understanding of each other's approach. It's important to note that Ryan is not in any way scared of John —

they often joke around with each other and it is often initiated by Ryan. But Ryan is also under no illusions about John's role as an authority figure in our house.

There are all kinds of models that blended families live under in defining parenting roles for stepparents. Some couples are perfectly happy living in scenarios where the biological parent is responsible for disciplining his or her own children. Our opinion is that separating disciplinary roles along biological lines does not take into account the messiness of daily life — there are simply going to be times where the stepparent must make discipline decisions in the absence of the biological parent. We do stress, again, that teenagers must be handled differently (the parent/friend approach); nevertheless, you can't play the "wait 'til your parent gets home" game forever, especially if you're dealing with younger teenagers.

Shona recently asked Ryan what he liked about John, and among some of the expected reasons (he sets up my computer games for me, he builds cool things, he makes great food), he very clearly stated that one of the things he appreciates about John is that he makes Shona happy. Shona and Ryan have always been very close. After all, he did have his mom to himself for six years, and it was important to him that his step dad and he were on the same team: Mom's.

There can be some jealousy and competition that arises in children *and* partners in blended families. This was certainly the case between Ryan and John; for the first two years, Shona had the sensation of being pulled in two directions whenever both wanted her attention. This is normal, both in adults and children, and John had the wisdom to understand that Ryan needed to continue to feel the security of his usual routines with his mom (spending time together every night before bedtime and going out alone together one night a week). It's not that he didn't sometimes feel that Shona spent more time with the kids than she did with him; he was just well aware that it was going to take some time for the new blended family to settle on some kind of routine that everyone was comfortable with and that met everyone's needs. Interestingly, John finds he is much more patient with Ryan when Shona is out of town on business because he recognizes that he is not feeling like Ryan is taking up too much of Shona's time. They actually gravitate to spending more time together when Shona is not around.

One way you can solidify your stepchildren's perception that you are all on the same team is to not argue or disagree with your partner in front of the children, and especially never about discipline issues. It is natural for your own children to defend you in a conflict or to try to co-opt your support when they are in a dispute with their stepparent. Even if you heartily disagree with your partner's position, don't even think about taking him or her up on it when the child is present. You will just be setting your partner up for failure and leaving your children with the impression (rightly so) that you will defend their interests against the stepparent. This is a recipe for disaster in your partner and your blended family relationships.

Our different parenting styles became a key issue in coming to an agreement over how we were going to parent Ryan. Shona had been experiencing behavioral issues with Ryan at home and at school. Ryan isn't a bad kid but he is very bright with a strong personality and an almost innate sense of self-esteem. While these are all wonderful qualities, it can be very challenging to parent a young child and guide him or her through the learning required to channel those qualities in a mature fashion. Shona often found it very difficult to do the tough stuff because she felt sorry for him. Like many parents, it's hard to discipline your child and know he or she will feel bad. It's important to remember that, whether you're a stepparent or an intact family parent, it's your job sometimes to do the tough stuff. Children are going to feel bad or unhappy when you discipline them for bad behavior —and they should. After all, this is how we help children develop a conscience. If we're not willing to point out the difference between right and wrong for our children, who will?

Add to the mix the guilt divorced parents often feel, and it can be doubly difficult (we'll talk more about guilt issues later).

Often Shona would give Ryan the benefit of the doubt when he had clearly shown that he knew exactly what he was doing. John, on the other hand, would feel she was being too soft and was not as inclined to give Ryan the benefit of the doubt as often. After all, he had already been through it three times with the older children and, coupled with his training in child development, was a lot wiser to the tricks of the trade children generally employ.

In our parenting partnership, we have noticed there is a distinct difference in what we call our disciplinarian default — John's default is "no," Shona's default is "yes." So whenever the children approach John for something, his immediate response tends to be on the negative side while Shona thinks in terms of there being no good reason why not. John's perspective on the "no" default can be broken down into four main elements:

1.   Children always want more. No matter how much you give them, they'll be back later asking for something else. The world is not a place of an endless supply of whatever they want, and we prepare them better for handling that world when they understand this. Building a sense of entitlement in our children does them no good.

2.   Saying no gives the parent time to think about the issue and decide what is in the best interests of the child. Our experience is that if you say "maybe," or "I'll think about it," children view that as invitation to continually harass you about it until you give in.

3.   It's a safer position when a parent is under pressure. Children are very clever when it comes to handling their parents — they size up the situation and pick the time to approach you wisely. If you're in a good mood and feeling generous with the world, they know it's in their best interest to ask you now for what they want.

It doesn't make them sneaky or manipulative, it just makes them human.

4.   It makes the child more cautious about asking for things. If the parent always or often says yes, it will reinforce the child's belief that he or she will receive a positive response most of the time. It's not that positive responses are bad, it's more about the kind of expectation you create in your child's mind.

Shona sees the logic of John's "no" default, but that doesn't always mean she can live it herself. Over time, however, her ability to say no has improved a lot.

After much trial and tribulation, we have learned two main things about each other and how we can jointly parent successfully: 1. We have to talk about everything, every night, consistently until we reach a comfort level and understanding about each other's style and what is effective. 2. Part of that involves being willing to admit our weak areas as a parent and allowing the other parent to fill that gap. Shona admits she can be way too soft and trusting at times, frequently erring on the side of giving the kids the benefit of the doubt, based on the premise that they are basically good kids with no ill intentions. For his part, John admits that sometimes he can be too strict and is rarely inclined to give the kids the benefit of the doubt, based on the premise that he knows what he was like as a kid as well as his experience with the older children. We have settled into a comfortable parenting style that honors both of our approaches, but at the same time, we can both point out (calmly) when the other person's natural style is not useful in a particular situation.

Family traditions

A common source of conflict —and therefore an area that requires careful visioning —is honoring family rituals and traditions. By the time you inherit your stepchildren, there are no doubt entrenched views of what happens on Christmas, birthdays, and other major holidays —and they may be quite different from your ideas about what is appropriate.

We probably ran into fewer of these issues than a lot of blended families by virtue of the fact that John grew up in a very austere religion where major holidays and birthdays were not celebrated. Consequently, he —and his children (although he had left the religion long before the children were old enough to know) —had very few firmly planted models about holiday and other traditions. Recognizing that he has very few traditional notions about those kinds of events, John generally bows to Shona's customs. He has, however, introduced the idea that the new family should create some new customs of their own that only the blended family shares.

One example is every Christmas since Kate was two, we have travelled to a nearby resort town in the mountains to purchase special ornaments for our tree. Ryan and Kate are each allowed to pick out an ornament and we pick one each as well. When Rudie, Tim, and Paul-Andrew have been around, they have sometimes come with us. The result is the creation of a Christmas tree theme that is unique to our blended family —not one that came from either of the previous families.

There have been some issues, however. The first one that showed up was a material issue around Christmas presents. Shona grew up in a family where children received numerous presents. While they were generally not too expensive there was volume! This volume included presents from Santa Claus, parents, grandparents, siblings, and even aunts and uncles. Because many of Shona's relatives live overseas, she would often receive money in lieu of gifts but her relatives sent the money with the express wish that she purchase gifts for her children with it.

The first Christmas we all spent together illuminated for Shona just how differently the Penton family handled things. It had been their tradition to receive basically one present with a handful of smaller gifts from siblings. What this meant was numerous gifts under the tree for Ryan and Kate (when you added in all the relatives' stuff), and not very many for John's older kids. The difference escaped no one.

One thing this situation led Shona to do was reflect on the ingrained notion that she needed to purchase gifts for the children with all the money she received. Her parents were of the opinion —and had taught Shona and her sister —that if someone sent you money with the express wish to purchase something, you had a duty to honor their wishes. The result was an overabundance of presents under the tree, which had never really struck Shona until it was pointed out to her by her eldest stepson. In truth, she was rather embarrassed by the whole thing.

On the other side was the fact that John's family was often exactly the opposite, sometimes failing to purchase each other gifts at all. Although she admits to a distaste for the commercialization of Christmas and has greatly toned down her present-buying habits, Shona had a really hard time with that approach.

Christmas traditions are things that, logically or not, we have lived with and accepted since childhood. They are filled with emotions and values that are sometimes difficult to understand. Your best approach when it comes to such traditions (or lack thereof) is to just accept them and move on. We'll go into the issue of acceptance in a much bigger way later on.

Besides the present part of major holidays and birthdays, there was an emotional tradition that Shona found hard to let go of when dealing with John's children and extended family. At the beginning of our blended family life together, Shona struggled all the time to include everybody in everything —if Tim couldn't attend John's birthday dinner, she felt guilty that somehow she was being a bad step mom. She was very concerned that John's children didn't feel like he had moved on to a new family and therefore they were less important. What she didn't realize was that she had an internal expectation that everyone would be together for major events and, allowing for times when they were at their mother's —which she fully understood and accepted —she often felt confused and offended when they failed to make plans or show up for events.

For their part, they were merely continuing with their tradition of not really marking any major holiday or birthday with any kind of ceremony, so it all felt okay to them. Not once have they been offended when we planned something they couldn't necessarily attend during major holidays. They have always felt free to be there or not. Shona actually thinks there is something really nice about that relaxed approach, which is in stark contrast to the sometimes duty-driven events of her own family of origin.

To ensure that she doesn't spend a lot of time on holidays feeling distressed she has finally come to the conclusion that she needs to make whatever plans she and John want for them and the two younger children, and if the others show up — good. If they don't — that's fine too.

The bottom line is we recommend you find some kind of happy compromise between you and your partner's family traditions. If one family traditionally has turkey at Christmas but the other has lamb, have one on Christmas Eve and one on Christmas Day, or have both on the same day. If your family traditionally opens presents on Christmas Eve but your partner just can't accept that his children will wake up on Christmas morning with nothing under the tree, then allow certain presents to be opened on Christmas Eve, and leave the rest for the next morning. If a church service is traditional in her family at Easter and your family never went, go to the church service. Our default mechanism is that if one family had a tradition or strong feeling around a certain thing, and the other family didn't, go with the desire of the partner who has the tradition. After all, if you never did it and you don't particularly care, what does it matter? The added bonus is that you'll make your partner and his or her children happy, and who knows? Maybe you'll grow to like the tradition and you and your kids will embrace it as your own too.

Of course, this becomes even more complicated if you and your partner have different religious faiths and cultures. We have, however, seen many wonderful approaches to blending holidays and traditions with Chanukah being celebrated as well as Christmas; Ramadan and Eid happen as matter of course in the family as well as Easter and Thanksgiving. When you think about it, what better place is there for a child to learn tolerance and embrace diversity than within his or her own family?

Part 3

Ingredient #2: Acceptance

Dear God, I pray for patience...and I want it right now.[1]
- Oren Arnold

Chapter Six

Paving the Road with Good Intentions

What is guilt? Guilt is the pledge drive constantly hammering in our heads that keeps us from fully enjoying the show.[1]
- Dennis Miller

The second ingredient in our Recipe for Blended Family Success® is Acceptance. To give you a clear understanding of what we mean by Acceptance, which we will go into in a lot of detail in the next few chapters, we need to start at the very beginning of our relationship.

When Shona met John and learned he was a single, custodial parent to three teenagers, alarm bells went off in her head. There was no way, she thought, she was ever going to get involved with someone who had that many children —and teenagers as well! Part of that came from her own experience of being a single parent and knowing how much work it was, part of it came from her knowledge that parenting teenagers is incredibly challenging, never mind parenting teenagers that aren't yours. Finally, she just couldn't picture herself being part of a family with that many children.

On his side, John's reaction to facing the prospect of potentially becoming a parent to a five-year-old when his own children were so close to leaving home was somewhat less negative. Although looking forward to the freedom of not having day-to-day responsibility for parenting, John was so enchanted by Shona that he was willing to accept the cost of doing it all over again.

Looking back on it now, he realizes he was somewhat naïve about how much energy he would need to expend by having a second family with young children. The older you get, the less energy you have to provide active parenting. There is some compensation, however, in that John is able to use his experience and previous mistakes to avoid the development of certain issues with the two younger children. We have reflected many times since then on how life sends you whatever it sends you —regardless of your personal wishes in the matter!

Having made the decision to blend families, we started out our lives together with a host of good intentions: we're all going to get along well, we'll be able to resolve any conflict, it can't be that much different than a nuclear family, I'm sure we'll figure it out, etc. Good intentions are a great place to start. After all, the very fact that you have made the commitment to blend your family with your new partner's is an admirable thing all on its own. You know there are other children involved, you know there are challenges ahead, but you have *willingly, consciously*, agreed to do it.

Hopefully, the first week lives up to all of your expectations (if not, skip these introductory paragraphs and go right to the issues). If you're really lucky, the first month will live up to your expectations. If you have the most incredible luck of anyone on the entire planet, the first three months will live up to your expectations. No matter how long the honeymoon lasts, however, reality is going to set in sooner or later, and you will begin to experience all of the trials and tribulations of blended family life. It may or may not comfort you to know that every blended family goes through a honeymoon stage, only to be rudely awakened from the pleasant, but unrealistic fantasy. In any case, forewarned is forearmed, as they say, and before you reach the end of that road paved with good intentions (and believe us —you'll know *exactly* when that is!), read on to learn of the purgatory that awaits you. Just keep in mind, however, that purgatory is a *temporary* state of affairs, and all of this will pass when you apply a little skill, ingenuity, and a lot of tenacity.

Common challenges for blended family parents

When the honeymoon passes, what kinds of things will you find yourself resisting, arguing about, and generally getting yourself discombobulated over? Here's a list of our initial resistances (some are specific to John, some are specific to Shona, some applied to both of us). They are in no particular order and the list is by no means exhaustive. We're sure you can add a lot more to this list based on your personal experiences. This will get you started, though.

Please keep in mind that feeling any or all of these things is perfectly normal. You are not an evil human being because you feel resentment or anger. The trick is what you ultimately do with these feelings —we'll get to that later. For now, let's just review some of the most common issues.

1. Being financially responsible for someone else's children

Before we get into some of the challenges around being financially responsible for your partner's children, we'd like to say a quick word on finances in general. Neither of us is an expert on financial affairs, but we have learned one important lesson: you must do what works for both of you. There is no one right way to handle financial affairs in a couple or a blended family. If you're not sure of the best way to proceed, we recommend you talk to a financial counselor or planner. Many issues around finances depend on your money personality —how you view money and the saving, spending, and management of it. There are numerous books out there than can help you make good decisions, and we've noted some of them in the *Resources* section. Make sure you read some of them and talk to each other about the money rules in your blended family, if not before you move in together then very soon afterward.

Whether you decide to pool your family's money or keep separate accounts, sooner or later the financial demands of one or all of your partner's children are going to affect you. If you pool your resources, you may find yourself resenting any number of things: your partner has more kids than you do (or your partner just plain has kids). Your partner's kids are older and therefore their financial demands are bigger. Your ex or your partner's ex doesn't provide any or is sporadic with child support payments. Your partner spends more on his or her kids than he or she does on yours. You and your partner have conflicts over how to handle money, etc.

If you decide to keep your money separate, you may find you resent that one person contributes less to joint expenditures because he or she has more kids or different spending habits. You may resent that you have to pay out child support but your spouse doesn't so he or she has more disposable cash than you. Your partner is frequently late with the agreed-upon share of the mortgage, groceries, whatever. If you have a child together, how do you equitably distribute that financial burden while taking the other kids into account? You may resent that your partner makes more money than you do so can do more fun things with his or her disposable cash, etc.

Money issues figure prominently in healthy, happy nuclear families, so it's no surprise they affect blended families as well. As with everything else, you have the added complexity of multiple and differing needs from biological and nonbiological children to deal with on top of the normal issue of how couples deal with income.

2. Giving up control and care of personal and prized possessions

John had a lot more practice with this because he had more kids and they were almost grown. While Shona had become accustomed to sharing her house with Ryan, the introduction of the three older children provided her with unexpected nervousness over issues like use of the car. Many times, they solved the issue by having John's kids use his car, but it didn't always work out that neatly, and Shona was surprised to discover that any time one of John's kids used her vehicle, she worried about it. It's not that she thought they would wilfully do any damage to her vehicle, it's just that prominent in her mind was the way she used to handle her parents' vehicle when she was a teenager. Of course, she was also worried about someone getting injured or worse.

The objective data was that both Paul-Andrew and Rudie were good drivers (and continue to be), but putting three tons of very expensive metal in the care and control of two kids under twenty took some getting used to. As for Tim, he had not yet gotten his driver's license so there was the added stress of occasionally taking him out for driving practice in the only new car Shona had ever been able to afford. Nail-biting times to be sure. Shona learned that you never have a clear picture of your sense of ownership over material things you have worked hard to get until you have to relinquish them to someone you don't trust to have your best interests at heart. (It never once bothered her to relinquish her vehicle to John.) It's somewhat different than giving your car to your own teenage children whom you have accepted will use your car as they grow older.

And the inevitable did happen. Rudie had a couple of car accidents, both of which she escaped from without injury and paid for with her own hard-earned money. In the short run, this only exacerbated Shona's nervousness about the children's safety and giving up expensive, hard-earned possessions to their responsibility. In the long run, she learned a lot about Acceptance.

It's not just the big things, however, that cause you consternation. Even small things like carpets getting stained due to careless attention got under Shona's skin. Anyone with children knows that your attachment to such material things naturally wanes over time because if it didn't, you'd be spending your entire days worrying about marks on the wall or scratches on the table. Kids are messy, unconsciously destructive, and generally teach you that things are expendable and ultimately unimportant. Shona figures she would have learned this lesson anyway, step kids or not.

3. Being responsible for someone else's children and the time that requires

John went from having a fairly independent lifestyle with three almost-grown, independent teenagers to living in a house with a demanding six-year-old, a new partner with time demands of her own, and all the work of a new baby long after he thought his baby days were over. He was used to and needed a fair amount of solitude, something he got a lot of with busy teenagers coming and going. Sometimes, when we've had a particularly stressful day due to the demands of the younger children, he'll jokingly comment, "And to think I was almost done…I could see the end in sight!"

Shona also had adjustments to make in transitioning from a fairly quiet house and independent lifestyle living with just her son to a house full of big, noisy people with adult demands. Sure, she had been busy with Ryan during the days, but after he was in bed she had plenty of time to herself to pursue her interests, turn the lights out when she wanted, or hire a sitter and go to a movie with friends. She was quite relieved that Ryan was out of diapers, in school, and developing his own life. Then along came John, three teenagers, and a new baby. Shona also enjoyed having some solitude at least on a weekly basis, and she found it overwhelming to have so many people interacting with her in the house, not to mention the time constraints a brand new baby put on her.

As parents in a blended family, both of us wanted to ensure we nurtured all the relationships involved to some extent, which basically meant less alone time for us, less time with our biological kids, not as much time as we'd like with our step kids to build a relationship, and feeling like we were run ragged trying to keep up with varied time demands from every quarter.

4. Dealing with ex-partners

If you're really lucky and have worked hard, you have an amiable relationship with ex-partners who are also the parents of your children. We've certainly seen those kinds of relationships. But we don't want to be all sweetness and light about this —our observation is, even if you have a reasonably friendly relationship with your ex-partner, it's still a very real complicating factor in managing a life with your blended family.

When we first became a blended family, we sought out resources to help us manage this sometimes volatile issue. We didn't find much to help us and the one book we did locate assumed that everyone was willing to work together. This hasn't always been the case with us and it's certainly not the case among many of our friends.

In John's case, his ex-wife lives quite a distance away so the vast majority of dealings with her were conducted over the phone. Generally speaking, there weren't many conflicts, but when they did arise, they weren't pretty and were quite complex to deal with. John has a skilled way of communicating that would calm the waters pretty quickly, but Shona occasionally resented this as she felt John's ex should depend on her new partner to help her resolve any feelings and reactions before dealing with John.

Many of the issues seemed to revolve around Shona's relationship with John's children. When someone else who isn't their parent is interacting with your children on a daily basis and you're not, there is bound to be some sensitivity around it. While understanding the feelings behind it, Shona often felt conflicted by the need to have her own rights and boundaries respected on the one hand and to keep the peace for the sake of the children on the other. In the end, Shona felt it was best to defer all those issues to John as the situation became highly emotionally charged at times. It's not ideal but simply part of the complexity we must accept that goes along with living in a blended family.

One couple we know have had a particularly challenging time dealing with his ex-wife. She will frequently cancel the children's visits, block her ex-husband from seeing them, and not inform him of important events going on in the children's lives until the last minute, if at all. No amount of trying to talk to her and work out an arrangement they can all live with has worked. At one point he decided to bypass his ex-wife and give his children (aged four and seven) little notebooks with all of his phone numbers in them, telling them they could phone him any time a big event was coming up so he could arrange to come. It worked well for about a month until his ex-wife found out about it and banned her children from using the phone. Currently, our friend has decided that, rather than continue arguing with his ex-wife, which causes great distress for his children, he will do the best he can to get information from the children on their activities and just simply hope they know he wants to be there. This is a decision of Acceptance on his part, a difficult but ultimately wise decision. Here's why.

One of the things he has learned over time, as have we, is the worst thing you can do is fight with and criticize your ex-spouse in front of the children. No matter how tempting it is for him to tell his children that the reason he has missed some of their events is because their mother didn't tell him about them, he never says a word. He is hoping that, as they grow older, they will witness her actions for themselves and come to their own conclusions about their mother's behavior.

This has certainly been the case in our family. There has been a long-running situation with one of our ex-spouses that has been frustrating and infuriating at times. But we never let the children know about it, and with the exception of the youngest, all of them have concluded (accurately) for themselves the real nature of the situation; we didn't need to say a word. When an ex-spouse is causing difficulty, no matter how tempting it might be for you to vent or explain to your children, resist the urge. The absolute best thing you can do is model positive and kind behavior, for your own exemplary behavior with their other parent will present a contrast that will not escape them. Trust us — they will recognize the difference. Time is on your side.

For Shona, there haven't been too many issues with Ryan's father. Generally speaking they get along well and relations are cordial. In recent years, there have been more complicated issues to work out, however, as Ryan's dad has remarried and had more children with his new wife. That has caused some irritations on both sides over having to coordinate our family schedule with their family schedule, but so far it hasn't been anything we haven't been able to work out.

One issue that can be sensitive is occasions when one or both of you have to spend time with your ex-spouse. When Ryan was still a young child, there were times when Shona needed to spend time with her ex-husband at events like Ryan's soccer games, parent-teacher interviews, meeting to plan Ryan's annual vacation/visitation schedule, etc. While Shona's ex was very open to and welcoming of John's involvement in all of those events, John couldn't always be there; he couldn't help feeling a little resentful of the time Shona spent with the her ex and Ryan —and therefore away from him.

That challenge has eased somewhat since Ryan has become a teenager himself. He is exerting much more of his own will and desires when it comes to visitation and interactions with his father's family and how our lives are affected. To a certain extent, that has removed the burden on both of his parents to be as closely involved as before. In another way, it makes it more complicated as Shona and her ex are trying to manage the new situations and demands brought on by their son's transition to life as a teenager. At this point, we don't necessarily know what the answers will be —a lot of it has to be taken one day at a time and with a lot of communication.

We know that there are a number of parents out there who experience very distressing and manipulative behavior on the part of their ex-spouses. In one particularly distressing situation, a friend of ours experienced his ex-wife staging a years-long 'smear campaign' with his children, effectively convincing them that their father was an evil man and they shouldn't have anything to do with him. He became distressed and despondent and unfortunately, did not react in ways that endeared him to the legal system. His ex-wife used his reactions to her advantage in keeping the children away from him. For many years he had no contact with his children, a sad situation for a man who dearly loved and wanted to be with them. Happily, three out of four of his children have re-established contact since reaching adulthood and they are having some wonderful times getting to know their father for who he really is.

If you find yourself in a similar situation, we urge you to seek legal assistance before doing anything rash. In desperation to see our children, we don't always think straight when that right is being denied. Laws governing custodial and visitation rights have changed considerably over the past number of years in the United States and Canada, shifting away from granting one parent exclusive right to say where and when children will be with the other parent. No matter how difficult the wait is for you, find out what your rights are and seek appropriate assistance.

5. Differences in family rituals

As mentioned previously, we don't encounter a huge amount of these with the exception of some holiday and birthday traditions. Day-to-day rituals do cause some consternation from time to time, however. For example, in Shona's mind dinnertime is an opportunity for lively discussion of the day's and world events; her family always viewed dinnertime as the chance hear what everyone was doing/learning, how they felt about it, and even to engage in heated but friendly political debates. John seemed to be much more introverted and preferred to have quiet meals where a lot of discussion didn't happen. Shona had some difficulty getting used to this.

When she brought it up with John, it turned out that it wasn't that he didn't like dinner table discussion. It was just that he found the discussions were often dominated by the children and pointed out that adults needed a chance to contribute at the dinner table too. Again, we were dealing with an issue of balance —in frustration, John's default on dinner table discussion became "no," while Shona's remained "yes." Eventually, we found that undergoing some frustration in the process of teaching our children how to have appropriate and respectful contributions to discussions helped a great deal.

Another issue with dinner is that Shona felt it was the only time of the day everyone was able to be together; consequently she felt people should try their utmost to be there. If the phone rang, it would not be answered during that period. This particularly frustrated Rudie, who would just about pop a vein in her head straining to keep herself from running for the phone when it rang during dinner. John honors this wish of Shona's not to have the phone answered during dinner, not so much from a family-togetherness point of view, but because he considers it an intrusion on the family's quiet time.

6. Pre-existing family conflicts

As John's kids were almost grown, they had a lot more history with their dad than Shona had with her kids. As is normal for adolescents and young adults, they may have resented or held grudges against their parents for real or imagined wrongs, and when they insisted on recycling them again and again, Shona felt duty bound to rush to John's defence. He discussed all of the situations with Shona at some point, and she often felt like the older kids either didn't have all the facts (sometimes they didn't), or simply failed to understand that no parent is perfect and that parenting sometimes means tough choices your kids don't like. Intellectually she knew she couldn't expect that level of mature understanding from teenagers, but emotionally she felt they were being unfair to their father (who she thinks, after all, is the most wonderful person in the world!).

One example of this was when one of John's sons chose not to graduate from high school with good marks. We say chose because this is exactly what happened —he was a bright young man who, despite repeated discussions with John, refused to apply himself. He said that he was having a good time and didn't want to worry about marks —he could worry about that and things like college later. John felt it was time to draw a boundary for himself and make it clear that the world didn't owe his son a living. (Where have you heard that before?!) He told his son that he would respect his decision, but the consequence of that decision would be no financial assistance from his dad if he had to attend upgrading classes to be able to pursue an education. His reasoning was clear: he was willing to support his son in completing high school while he was still of high-school age, but if he chose to squander that opportunity, then he would have to foot the bill for college preparation himself. John's son said that was fine by him.

The outcome was predictable. Graduation came and went and John's son graduated with enough credits to earn him a diploma, but his marks weren't adequate to earn him a spot at college. He left school and found a job that earned him a lot of money but at a high physical price due to the rough nature of the work. After several years, he decided that college was the place for him. Unfortunately, he had to do upgrading of high school courses for a period of time before he could even think about college. It was a tough time in his relationship with his dad. John was as good as his word and offered no support in helping his son get through it. Consequently, he worked at low-paying, part-time jobs at odd hours to put himself through upgrading, all the while carrying a lot of anger toward John. He mentioned it several times to Shona who, while feeling bad for him, also understood the reasoning behind John's decision and actions. He felt strongly that his children must be able to connect consequences to their own choices, and to be very clear that those consequences were explained to them before they made choices. If John hadn't followed through on his promise, he believed his son would not have learned a very important lesson.

It's now eight years later, and John's son has not only completed upgrading but has earned a university degree. He admits now that John's actions were the correct ones and, of course, is no longer angry. But sometimes it wasn't easy to deal with the negative behavior and attitudes that were directed at John.

The older they have become, the easier it is to discuss those past conflicts in an objective, mature manner. The older kids have naturally come to see their father as an individual but a flawed human being just like them —apart from being their dad.

7. Loss of control of your house, rules, family culture, etc.

While we've already touched on some of these issues, we felt it was worth reviewing a few concerns that may arise.

The best scenario in terms of living arrangements is to find a new family home that none of you has lived in before so no one has pre-existing ideas about "the way things are in this house." Unfortunately (and probably most of the time), that's not always possible.

In our case, John and Rudie moved into the house Shona was living in with Ryan. Then the baby came right away and, of course, the two older boys came and went on a regular basis. One of the things Shona had (fortunately) done as part of her decision to merge her life with John's was make a conscious decision to not show possessiveness over her house and the daily routine she and Ryan had established. This went a long way toward solving any issues over turf as it was important that John and Rudie feel that it was their house too.

This can be a huge issue, though, and if you haven't already talked about it or are already living the results of not addressing it, put on the top of your list to have a Family Meeting about it *today*. All family members simply *must* be able to view the house as their home, a place where they have the same rights and privileges as everyone else. Home needs to be a sanctuary for the entire family. There is just no room for having it any other way.

One thing that was problematic in terms of the house culture that we've already touched on is the fact that we had two kinds of families living in the house simultaneously. On the one hand, we had the young family with children who had early bedtimes and therefore so did the parents in order to get enough rest to meet the demands of early rising, feeding-through-the-night children, on top of work demands. On the other hand, we had the older family, with adolescents coming and going all the time, staying up on the phone and watching movies at all hours of the night, leaving lights on all over the house, not to mention being loud long after everyone else was in bed and foraging for food in the kitchen right next to our bedroom in the wee hours of the morning. Shona eventually invested in a set of ear plugs just out of sheer self-defence. While you can eventually find ways to meet everyone's needs, it is very challenging and can be frustrating until you can all figure out how to be respectful about what works best for everyone. The older children tried very, very hard to respect our young family needs even if they weren't always successful.

Another issue around house culture is the effect of your partner's grown children. As Shona viewed the two older boys as adults, she realized that she expected they would behave like adult guests visiting another adult's home when they came to stay. Not necessarily so. It took her a while to get used to the liberties she often felt they took in her home, like raiding the fridge the minute they arrived without even a word of hello, becoming proprietary about rooms and material things that didn't belong to them, and generally treating the home like it was theirs. She came to view that as quite flattering, for it meant they were as comfortable in the shared home as they would have been if it was only their dad's home, but it took a while to reframe the whole experience. It also required some firm boundary setting that will be discussed in Chapter Eleven.

8. Stepsibling conflicts

This could have been a lot worse for us than it was. Because the age differences among the children living at home fulltime were so large (baby, five, and fifteen at the beginning), there certainly wasn't a lot of rivalry among the children. Rudie needed to make some adjustments to having a younger brother underfoot all the time, which she generally did with a great deal of kindness and patience. Ryan had to learn what it was to have siblings at all, and while he had a slight adjustment to make to consider Rudie's privacy needs, he learned very quickly.

The biggest concern we had was the effect the new baby would have on everyone. Would the older children resent her as a symbol of Dad's new life and new family (separate from them)?

Would Rudie think she would be stuck babysitting all the time? Would Ryan, used to being an only child who commanded all of Mom's attention, resent her and the attention she would need?

These are all concerns to be aware of when you decide (or accidentally in our case!) to have another child together. Fortunately, none of these things came to pass. Kate is universally adored by all of her older siblings (and quite spoiled by them, we might add), and Ryan has always shown the utmost kindness and regard for his little sister. Lately, he is finding her quite an annoyance, which is normal for any older brother with a younger sister. Kate has now become sophisticated enough to know exactly what irritates Ryan and, of course, promptly does it.

We've seen many instances where children of blended families are, however, of the same age or very close in age, and it causes a lot of fighting and rivalry. The Brady Bunch was nice in theory but probably not realistic. When stepsiblings are close or identical in age, the level of conflict in your blended family will be high, at least at the beginning. They will no doubt have similar interests, covet the same toys and activities, and if teenagers, struggle with the same raging-hormones-that-cause-them-to-act-unreasonably-or-uncommunicatively at the same time.

We know one couple who got together and each had a nine-year-old; she had a daughter, he had a son. The havoc these children wreaked upon their parents' lives was intolerable. They fought from sun up to sun down and picked at each constantly over the slightest little things from dirty looks to touching knees when sitting next to each other. Part of the problem was neither child was used to having to share their parent with anyone nor had they experienced the need to share their toys, space and homes. The other part of the problem, and we think many of us forget this sometimes, is that the introduction of a new child may be quite threatening. What if my parent likes this child better than me? What if my new stepparent plays favourites with his or her own child?

Real or imagined, such perceptions tend to create defensive behaviors in children. Unable or unwilling to fully articulate such fears, young children and teenagers alike will seek out the nearest convenient target for their fears and anxiety — their new stepbrother or stepsister. It's a lot easier to focus your emotions on another child than it is to focus it on your new stepparent who, after all, is the partner your parent has chosen.

The key to managing the inevitable conflicts that will arise between stebsiblings close in age comes back to you as the parents. Consistent and strong parenting with a united front is critical, just as it would be when handling sibling conflict arising between your biological children. You cannot be tentative in these situations. You must require respectful treatment of each other, regard for one another's rights and needs, and a calm and thoughtful approach to conflict resolution. Resist the urge to defend your own despite being biologically hardwired to do so. This isn't about winning and making your child right; it's about creating a harmonious home where everyone feels their needs are met and rights are respected.

In this section on Acceptance and in the Communication section, you will find numerous tools and approaches to help you deal with stepsibling conflicts as well as tools you can teach them to use themselves to help them relate better to each other. These include creating a Family Pact, learning how to tune into each others needs, and coaching approaches to resolving conflict.

9. You experience resentment and unkindness from the stepchildren even though you have been unfailingly kind and respectful

This is a tough and, unfortunately, all too common scenario. Be prepared that, no matter how nice or considerate you are to your new stepchildren, it is going to take some time for this kind of behavior to cease (sometimes, it never does, which is why this section is all about Acceptance). Remember: you are the adult. You are often dealing with children who are hurt and resentful after divorce or for other reasons. They are often not able to articulate their feelings and will lash out at the nearest available and convenient target —you. They don't have the same kind of emotional investment in you as they do in their parents, and can easily come to view you as the reason for all their troubles.

None of that makes it any easier for you, of course. They may still be treating you badly and saying horrible things that hurt you just as much as it would anyone else. This is where the strength of your marital bond must kick in. Aside from seeking outside help and counseling as much as possible to help both the child and you adjust and communicate, your partner will play a pivotal role in helping the child accept (or at least respectfully tolerate) your presence. If your partner does not assume the role of making and defending a place for you in the family, not much will be resolved.

This did not happen with any of John's older children at all, which says a great deal about their character and kindness; it is within the adolescent and young adult group that this kind of scenario can be the most challenging. Apart from normal family irritations with one another, Shona and the three older children have been able to forge very amicable relationships.

Ryan is the one child who has expressed some instances of resentment, although they have been very minor. As we've mentioned, he made it clear, even at six years old, that he already had a father, thank you very much, and John was not it. He kept a somewhat cool, though amicable, distance between himself and John for quite a while, and only after several years did he begin to let his guard down somewhat. It appears to have resolved itself now that he understands he can do some dad things with John without being disloyal to his own father. They joke around regularly and have a few shared interests they have been able to develop a bond over.

If you're distressed that we said it took several *years*, don't be discouraged. This doesn't mean that it took years for them to get along. That's not true at all. We just meant it took years to develop increased and voluntary openness on Ryan's part.

Relationships are always and forever works in progress. What they are today are frequently not the same as they will be tomorrow. Children are infinitely flexible and will find ways to adjust and be happy if you allow them the space and respect to do so. It wouldn't have served us well at all to force a relationship between Ryan and John. Because of Ryan's strong personality he needed to have the freedom to arrive at things in his own time. As he heads into his teenage years, we are feeling positive about both of our abilities to communicate with him over the next few challenging years he will face.

10. You don't care for the other family's discipline approach

Again, we have touched on this in previous chapters, but it can be a huge area of conflict, especially if you have trouble talking about it and coming to some kind of agreement. If you have tried and failed to resolve this, family counselors or mediators can be extremely helpful in facilitating moving past the roadblocks. We recommend that you talk about it before you move in and/or have your own children together and especially recommend that you talk about it almost daily for the first couple of years — or at least until you are both sure you are speaking the same language.

That's what we did for the first two years and it has paid big dividends as we don't wonder very much anymore what the other person would do, if he or she would agree, and we don't have to talk about it nearly as much. One of the things that has helped us is that we have very similar sets of values regarding child rearing. That doesn't mean, however, that we didn't need to do a lot of talking.

As we've already discussed, John freely admits that he tends to err on the side of being more strict, and Shona freely admits that she tends to err on the side of being too soft. We try to balance each other off as much as possible and will often ask each other after a disciplining incident how the other person felt about how we handled it.

One thing we did have to deal with was Ryan's adjustment to John's style and to the fact that he had another adult in his life who was going to play a disciplinary role. All of the blended family books we have read have offered some version of the idea that you can totally expect to play a discipline role with young children, but that role should be introduced gradually. That's certainly what we felt was the best way to proceed and it took about two years before John assumed a disciplinarian role with Ryan equal to Shona's.

Again, as we've already discussed, one of the tough parts about becoming an instant parent to a teenager is the role ambiguity associated with it. Are you a parent? Kind of, but it's maybe a little less than a parental role. Are you a friend, then? Again, kind of, but it's maybe a bit more than a friendship role. It's a tough line to walk and you are constantly asking yourself what is the right role to play in any given situation. In reading about this issue in other books, many stepparents have chosen to adopt a teacher/mentor kind of role with their teenaged stepchildren, and while we don't think that quite captures it, we would say that it generally captures the role that Shona carved out for herself in Rudie's life. With the two older boys, her role is certainly more on the friend side given the fact they didn't live with us fulltime.

Interestingly, Shona found this role to be inadequate when one of the older boys did move in with us, and if it had continued past the few months over which it did occur, she would have felt the need to redefine how they were interacting. It often struck Shona that he seemed to expect some kind of parenting behavior on her part even though he was twenty, whereas Shona wanted to deal with him purely on an adult-to-adult basis.

11. Believing that because your partner's children are grown and out of the house, they won't have an influence on your life and your relationship with your partner

This is an assumption that Shona certainly made about John's two older children, Paul-Andrew and Tim. No matter what you think, the grown children of your partner are definitely going to influence the nature of your blended family relationships. We've already addressed most of those influences in previous sections.

As mentioned, one of the things you may discover as a stepparent of grown children is that you want to ensure the first family doesn't feel left out of the second family. This may be bigger in your mind or bigger in theirs, but it is an element to consider. In our case, Paul-Andrew and Tim have never shown any indication of feeling left out, and it would distress Shona greatly if they ever did feel that way. She has tried very hard to include them in most things the family does; even if they can't make it she at least feels she needs to offer an invitation.

One issue Shona failed to anticipate involved the unexpected financial demands placed upon the family as a result of either unfortunate circumstances or simply irresponsible choices on the part of the newly independent children. Again, it is quite normal for young adults living on their own for the first time to get themselves into financial jams due to lack of experience, but it can be particularly stressful when you are having a hard time budgeting for the kids who are still at home. On several occasions Shona was ready to pull her hair out because, as the money manager of the family, she would have the monthly budget nailed down to the last penny and one of the grown up kids would have a financial crisis. There would go any extra money we had, which meant not going out for dinner —just the two of us —and worse, going into further debt to help bail out the young adult.

Shona says the worst part about it was feeling like her security was under threat all the time because she simply couldn't anticipate when the grown kids' lack of planning would become our emergency. Young adults are also notorious for borrowing money and then honestly forgetting to pay you back, or when they do pay you back, being off by hundreds of dollars in terms of what they remember borrowing from you. It's not that we bailed them out every time —we were willing to let them suffer financial hardship resulting from their own decisions —but there were still times when we had no choice but to put aside our own needs and help out.

Additionally, they will expect all kinds of help in other ways and essentially treat you like a de facto parent, but not consistently be willing to accord you the official status of it. Shona remembers being out for dinner one night with one of the grown children and the baby, and a couple at the next table remarked on the age difference between the two children. When they asked how many children there were, and Shona said five, John's older child responded with great indignation that Shona could not take credit for having five children because, for one thing, she hadn't raised the older two, and for another, he was most certainly not a child. Aside from the fact that Shona could have debated the definition of child with him (she didn't), she was also quite offended that he seemed unable or unwilling to recall the things she had done to help him out, which clearly qualified as parenting, however modified.

❧

There are many other issues we discovered in the complexity of our stepfamily in addition to those listed above, but we think that gives you an example of the range you are looking at. We're sure you will have just as many unique to you and your situation. The important thing to remember is that, no matter what your challenges are, there are countless other blended families that are experiencing the same or similar ones. It doesn't make your family wrong or dysfunctional —it's just, realistically, the stuff you have to deal with.

Before we move on to approaches to addressing whatever your challenges are, there's one very important issue we feel we must address as it affects every single other issue: guilt. It can be a subtle and negative influence on the success of your blended family, and we feel no book about blended families is complete without addressing this nasty and destructive little monster.

That guilt thing

Besides all those and other situations you will experience and possibly resist, as parents of a blended family you get a double whammy because it's a safe bet you'll also be carrying a huge amount of guilt around. Guilt is a subtle, hidden, yet potentially powerful force in practically every blended family that, left unaddressed, can have a serious effect on your ability to be successful.

The thing you need to know about guilt, however, is that a lot of it is misplaced and undeserved. We'll talk about how to deal with it later. For now, let's take a look at the top ten on the guilt hit parade for parents in blended families. Please note we're not saying any of this is appropriate guilt at all, it's just the usual line-up of things we like to beat ourselves up over. You might feel some or all of these things. You might feel a whole range of different things. But we bet you're busy feeling guilty about *something* in your blended family.

1. You got divorced in the first place

Now your kids come from a broken home (does anybody actually use that expression anymore?) and you have ruined any potential they had to lead happy, productive lives. If you never did marry/live with your child's biological parent, then you may suffer similar guilt over never having provided them an opportunity to have a close (or closer) relationship with that person. This applies even if that person is horribly evil or willingly chose not be involved in his or her child's life, which in no way eliminates *your* personal sense of guilt for having been involved with that person in the first place.

2. Now you're making your child/children live with another adult/family they're not related to

Adding insult to the injury you have already caused them by getting divorced or never getting married in the first place,

you are forcing them to cope with a stepparent they don't love —
maybe don't even like — plus whatever other children that person
is bringing to the blended family. They're going to experience
conflicts, share their house (or even their room), and just generally
not have you to themselves any more. Which leads to...

3. How can you be so selfish, putting your own needs before your child's?

We know you're in love and this is a second (or third, or
fourth, or even fifth) chance at happiness, but you should be
thinking of your child first. What if he or she is uncomfortable?
— doesn't want to change? — is unhappy?

4. You'll have less time to devote to your child/children

Your children will have to get used to the fact that you want
to spend time with your new partner and also build a relationship
with his or her children. There will also be new family events and
traditions that they're not used to and may not like.

5. You don't actually love your new stepchildren

You evil, evil person. How can you not love these innocent
human beings who, through no fault of their own, have had
to endure their parents splitting up and now have to welcome
you as parent? Shame on you. Even considering that the little
darlings have behaved perfectly hideously toward you from
Day One, you should love them. You're the adult, after all. Or
worse...

6. You have moments when you wish there were no children at all

Your evilness continues. Never mind that you have days
like this with your *own* children — isn't it horrible that you
harbor these thoughts about your partner's children? If you're

a woman, you fantasize sometimes that you are the baroness in the *Sound of Music* who wants to convince the hapless Captain von Trapp that all of his children should be shipped off to a boarding school (never mind that they had money and you don't). If you're a man, it's hard to know what you fantasize about as literature and music is packed full of evil stepmother figures but is relatively devoid of evil stepfather figures. Nevertheless, you may feel less than charitable toward your partner's children some days, which makes you just as evil.

7. How can you put your ex-partner through the pain of watching someone else raise/help raise his or her children?

Didn't you put them through enough already by leaving the relationship and taking the kids with you? It must be so difficult for him or her to stand by and watch your new partner play a big parenting role in your child's life, knowing it should be him or her who's spending that time.

8. How can I put my new partner through the pain and perhaps the ordeal of raising my children?

This is especially distressing when your children don't like your new partner and have done everything they can to make his or her life miserable. He or she is being so kind and understanding and all your children do is cause him or her problems. Variations on this could be: my partner had no children and now I'm putting this burden on him or her, or my partner's children are grown and now he or she has to start all over again with mine.

9. It will feel disloyal to my new partner to have to spend time with my old partner due to parenting responsibilities

There's nothing like having kids to ensure that, no matter how long you've been divorced, you will have to keep dealing with the person you long ago decided you would prefer not to see again. You have to spend a lot of time with your ex-partner due to custody/visitation arrangements and the kids' activities. You sure hope your new partner knows there's nothing going on —that you're doing it because you have to for the kids.

10. How can I live with and raise someone else's children when I don't even get to do that with my own?

One thing that many men feel guilty about is when their children from a previous marriage are with the ex-spouse and they can't actively parent them on a daily basis. At the same time, they have daily interaction with and parenting duties for children who are *not* biologically theirs. This sets up a no-win scenario in the father's mind: he feels guilty about not being able to actively parent his own children, and he may feel doubly guilty because he has those feelings while carrying a serious responsibility to his stepchildren. He may believe his conflicting feelings mean he isn't being fair to either set of children.

All of this, of course, applies to women as well, but it is more frequently a male experience.

❧

No doubt you have other things going on in that private whipping room in your head, but you get the picture. One of the biggest challenges you are going to face as a stepparent is not allowing all of these guilt feelings to affect first your relationship with your partner, and second, your relationship with all of the children.

When you add up all the challenges facing blended families and put them together with the numerous guilt issues, it doesn't paint a pretty picture, does it? You're probably thinking it looks pretty bleak right now. With all that stuff coming at you, how are you ever going to be successful and happy in your blended family? We're going to cover that very soon, but before we do, we felt it was very important to address something we call the Super Parent Syndrome.

Dealing with the super parent syndrome

Feeling like you need to be a super mom or super dad could easily be number eleven on the blended family guilt hit parade, but it's such a big one we felt it deserved a more detailed discussion than the other ten items. Here's what we mean when we refer to the Super Parent Syndrome.

As Shona has become a more experienced parent, one of the things she has happily realized is that there are a thousand different models of what a good mom looks like. It was a long process, though, for she found herself frequently feeling guilty for being a career woman and often resisted the fact that she would rather be somewhere else than looking after her children at home for an extended period of time. She loves her children just as intensely as other parents do, but she has come to accept and understand that neglecting her own needs and interests is harmful to her children's growth, development, and well-being. She is a much happier, patient, and loving mom when she is happy in her own life in terms of her relationship, her career, her interests.

Unfortunately, there still seem to be many taboos and rules around what constitutes the perfect mom. When Ryan was about six months old, Shona remembers watching a talk show where the theme was moms who go back to work immediately following the birth of their children *when they don't have to financially* instead of staying at home. One mom who had hired a live-in nanny to care for her children was harassed by the studio audience, hearing one audience member yelling accusingly, "Your children don't even know who their mother is!" The panel mom got very offended and replied in an angry tone, "My kids know *exactly* who their mother is." Shona remembers feeling incredibly guilty as she was considering returning to work at that time, not because she didn't love her son but because she felt the need for a different kind of stimulation that was better suited to her individual temperament.

While she has come to some kind of peace with her mom personality, she still sometimes feels surrounded by (and inferior to) the "perfect" mothers at Ryan's and Kate's schools when she volunteers for events. They are the kind of moms who volunteer *every* week at their children's school, who are able to stay at home fulltime, ferry their kids here there and everywhere, sew costumes, make crafts, and possess a seemingly inexhaustible reservoir of patience and energy, designing their entire lives around their children's growth, development, and activities. Reality is, none of these moms are perfect either, and everyone needs to make the best choices for themselves about how to be the best parent possible. There are no hard and fast rules and your children are not going to grow up to be axe murderers because you weren't there to supply the soda at the third-grade Valentine's Day party.

Then there are the parents who appear to be exhausted all the time from running their kids to every conceivable activity known to man. They have no time for themselves, let alone each other, but seem unable to let some activities go, fearing their children will not grow up to be well-rounded individuals. It is *not* going to permanently stunt your children's emotional growth to not be involved in baseball and football and soccer and swimming and music and dance and Scouts and piano and whatever else you think is important for them to be in this year. In fact, you may be harming their ability to develop the capacity to be creative, amuse themselves, be comfortable with solitude, and to just plain *be* instead of *do* all the time. By enrolling our children in so many activities, we may well be teaching them to be stressed-out overachievers before they even get to high school.

In our family, the policy is two activities at a time per child *maximum*. We do our utmost to ensure those activities coordinate with the activities of another child and that if they want to sign up for another activity there is only a short overlap. For example, Ryan enjoys swimming in the winter, so we have signed Kate up for swimming lessons at roughly the same time and evening as Ryan's. Now the family can coordinate around Monday and Thursday evening swimming lessons plus be there to cheer them on. Kate also takes piano lessons and is involved in gymnastics in the spring. Those take up two nights of the week. Sometimes, there is an overlap of two or three weeks when one activity is ending and another begins, but that's it. We cannot sustain nor are we willing to do children's activities four nights a week all the time. What all this means is that, generally speaking, we have two nights per week that are taken up with children's activities.

We know many families who are consistently busy four and five nights a week, plus time on weekends, keeping up with all of their children's activities. Frankly, in the interest of balance, meeting our own individual needs and our needs as a couple, and just plain sanity, we would never consider that. Our children are happy, healthy, engaged, and interested in lots of things. They are great readers and we do a variety of things on weekends like visiting the local science center or going to a movie, or just hanging out. We have a full and busy family life but we are not insanely racing from one activity to another every day. This means that if one of us wants to take an evening course, we can. This means that if one of us wants to go out with the girls or guys, we can. This means that if we want to go out alone as a couple, we actually have the time to do so (remember the notion of protected time and space as a couple?). Remember, you two are the reason your blended family is together in the first place. You have a right to a life and interests of your own.

Another aspect of the Super Parent Syndrome is the seeming need to provide all the material bells and whistles for the children. Take brand-name clothes, for instance. John would always refuse to buy his older kids brand-name clothes because he observed them getting caught up in peer pressure to wear expensive designer labels. Aside from the fact he couldn't afford them, it offended him that many of his teenagers' friends got whatever they wanted. John even refused to let his kids buy the clothes if they earned the money themselves for he saw it as a symptom of allowing their lives to revolve around the material aspects of life rather than the relational.

We could list a hundred things we see every day, from sixteen-year-olds getting brand new $50,000 trucks to ten-year-olds getting the latest version of whatever PlayStation, X-Box, or Game Cube that came out *this* month, or kids' cereal that's basically candy disguised as nutrition, to the latest $100 toy that your four-year-old will play with for five minutes before it breaks or the child loses interest (they'd rather play with the 99-cent box it came in anyway). The list goes on: backyard trampolines, regulation-sized soccer nets, mortgages way beyond our means, and vacations we'll spend the next three years paying for. It's okay to get your kids stuff (and it often feels good) but they're not going to grow up as crippled human beings simply because they didn't get to go to the latest teen idol's concert. Just because you can afford it doesn't mean your kids need it or that it is good for them.

If they do get all that stuff handed to them, there is a good chance they'll grow up with a sense of entitlement with no real appreciation for how most of the world lives. We recently heard a young starlet sum it all up for us. She had travelled to small-town America to be involved in the taping of a TV reality show. It involved her living with an average American family. Her comment? "I didn't know people actually had to work for their money."

You may well argue that all of these thoughts are true even if you don't live in a blended family —and you'd be right. It's just a lot of these things tend to get worse because we're living with crippling guilt over what we've done to our kids through our own choices. The truth is, whether you live in an intact family or a blended family, you can raise marvelous, responsible, committed, caring, contributing people without spending all of your disposable cash and time on them as children. And spending all that money and time isn't going to get rid of whatever guilt feelings you have about getting divorced and forcing your children to live in a blended family situation anyway.

❧

So what can you do about all this guilt? We believe these concerns, in addition to many others, can begin to be resolved by adopting an approach of Acceptance. Notice that we said *begin* to be resolved. Acceptance is your starting point for moving ahead, not the cure-all for your numerous frustrations. But what does Acceptance really mean and what does it look like in your blended family? The rest of this section will address just that issue. How can you accept that you're going to feel all of these things sometimes? How can you not let them affect your parenting and your partner relationship? How can you ease the burden of undeserved guilt you are heaping on yourself and clear the way for thoughtful approaches to life in your blended family? The first place to start is...

Stop shoulding on yourself

A lot of us set up our own personal torture chamber of shoulds and should nots, usually as a result of the ideas and values our own parents raised us with. The should scenario is the one most closely linked to your feelings of guilt: you should love your stepchildren, you should take your children to every activity they want, you should make dinner for your family every night...or what? What would happen if you didn't do those things one day? Does that automatically make you an unfit, uncaring, and irresponsible parent or person?

When Shona was a teenager, one of her parents' friends got divorced and then remarried. Then she got divorced again. Shortly after that second divorce, Shona was attending a social event at another friend's house with her parents, and the subject of the twice-divorced friend came up. There was a lot of tut-tutting and clucking with a final comment that "there must be something wrong with that woman." Shona's parents agreed. The lesson Shona took in? Getting divorced twice was shameful and indicated something was wrong with you.

Fast forward twenty years and there Shona was facing her second divorce. The memory of that long-ago social event came back along with the judgment her parents and their contemporaries had passed on their friend. Sure, times have changed and divorce is more common and acceptable. But it doesn't eliminate the social standards you grew up with and it doesn't keep you from passing the same judgment on yourself as you have heard your family members put on others.

So how can you deal with guilt and stop shoulding on yourself? Here's a three-step process.

1. Analyze your guilt

You may surprise yourself with what you discover. The first step is to take a certain situation over which you feel guilty and ask yourself, "Did I reasonably have any control over or influence on this situation?" Sometimes the answer is yes; sometimes the answer is no. Most of the time, it's not that simple —it's actually a combination of both.

For example, in the case of marriage, especially where children are involved, you want to feel like you made good decisions. But the truth is you're human. People change and grow all the time, and the simple fact is that people outgrow each other. Abusive relationships excepted, sometimes even when you have control and influence over the situation, it doesn't work out. In that case, your feelings of guilt are largely undeserved.

Here's another thought. When Shona reflects on her second marriage, she knows she had control and influence over certain parts of the situation, but she also knows that relationships are never a one-way street. She is well aware of what she is responsible for in the breakdown of her marriage. She is also well aware of what her ex-husband is responsible for. In the dark days during the looming end of her marriage, she recalls speaking with a friend about her efforts to work on the marriage. His comment? "Marriage is about two people giving one hundred percent, not fifty-fifty. If you're the only one giving one hundred percent it's not going to work."

We've always believed that the most important element of guilt is intention. Did you intend to do harm? Did you intend to end your relationship when you first got into it? Did you intend to hurt anyone? Did you purposefully and with forethought set out to hurt, manipulate, injure, insult or inconvenience anyone in any way? Did you not do the absolute best you could given the circumstances and knowledge you had at the time? If you can answer no to these questions, then you are torturing yourself unnecessarily with undeserved guilt. You are only human, after all. If your intentions were good and you did your best, move on.

If, on the other hand, you answered yes to any of those questions, don't despair. We are all works in progress. Sometimes we make poor choices and decisions because we don't have the skills to do anything else. In thinking back on her marriage, Shona is very clear on things she should have known better about but chose to do them anyway. She felt guilty for a long time about them. But here, too, is where analysis of the situation can help you.

In spending a lot of time trying to understand why she made certain choices in her marriage, Shona has been able to identify root causes of her choices. In other words, when you've done something you have cause to feel guilty about, the best thing you can do for yourself is dig below the surface behavior and figure out why. In Chapter Seven, we'll talk about a technique called the Five Whys that will help you through this process. Achieving understanding is the first step to growth and change. It can't change the choices you've already made, but it can help you make better choices next time. As the old saying goes "It's a waste of time to wish for a better past." The best you can do is work to ensure that you have a better future.

You will never be perfect. Accept it. When you've messed up, figure out why, take steps to ensure you never do it again, and then move on. No matter what your religious faith, like everyone else, you have the chance for redemption in the eyes of your maker. Can't you give yourself the same break? Stop "shoulding" on yourself and get on with the business of making better choices next time.

2. Identify where your opinions come from

The second technique to use in getting over "shoulding on yourself" is identifying whether the internal opinions and judgments you hold are actually yours, or merely the recycled opinions of others. It's amazing how much we think and react automatically without stopping to analyze why we hold the beliefs we do, or if we even actually hold those beliefs!

Here's an amusing and harmless example. Shona remembers once going house shopping with her first husband. They set up appointments to see numerous homes during the course of one day, all of which had a feature Shona said was very important to her: a big picture window in the living room. Despite the fact all of the houses had big picture windows, Shona didn't like any of them. No matter how nice the houses were, she would find some reason to turn them down. At the end of the day, her husband turned to her and said, "All of these houses had big picture windows and you didn't like any of them. What is it exactly that you want?"

Shona couldn't answer the question, but she did start thinking about it seriously over the next couple of days. A few days later, it finally dawned on her why she didn't like any of the houses. It was because she *didn't actually like* big picture windows at all! In fact, when she had lived in homes in the past with that kind of window, she had always felt a bit like she was in a fish bowl. She would be sure to close the curtains as soon as the sun went down because she didn't want to have the feeling of being watched by passers by.

So if she wasn't comfortable with picture windows, where did the notion come from? As it turns out, it came from her mother. While growing up, Shona and her family made frequent moves, and she has memories of her parents going house hunting with her mother saying, "I don't care about a lot of other things, but one thing I want for sure is a big picture window." Shona heard that opinion so often that she had absorbed it as her own, and never really questioned it as an adult. It took some intense self-analysis to identify the source, realize she didn't actually agree with the opinion, and then formulate her own.

We have often asked people in workshops questions like, "Why are you a Democrat? A Republican?" or "Why do you always buy Fords? Chryslers?" The vast majority of the time, the answer is some variation on, "My family has always voted that way," or "My daddy always swore by Ford." And so on. We don't mean to say that every opinion you hold is someone's else's, but we're willing to bet that when you start examining your opinions on a wide variety of topics, you will realize that you are really recycling the opinions of others, and you may not be sure if you actually believe that or not. That has certainly been the case in our lives.

John had a very educational experience with this kind of patterned thinking when he chose to leave the religion he was raised in. There were many things John grew up believing in because they were taught by his religion, including morals, values, and principles. Upon leaving the religion, one of the most freeing things he ever experienced was the right and the need to examine his beliefs —he never felt able to question such things before. Once he examined many of his key beliefs, he chose to accept and continue with many, while others he let go, realizing that they either didn't make sense to him anymore or he fundamentally didn't agree with them. The beauty of this was that John was free to make his own choice about his beliefs. The power of choice is an incredible one. Unfortunately, so many people don't take advantage of it because it's often easier to live unexamined lives given that questioning our beliefs can be really challenging or even threatening to our lifestyle.

This can be particularly damaging to you in a blended family situation when you hold beliefs that the only happy family is a family that never got divorced, or you find yourself reacting to actions the other family takes but can't really articulate why it bothers you. If you find yourself in those situations, take a hard look at your opinions and reactions and ask yourself if you really, truly believe that perspective. For Shona, the whole picture window thing was so disturbing to her that it led to a full-scale analysis over several years of many opinions she held near and dear. Upon reflection, she has, in some cases, completely reversed her opinions. She certainly no longer holds the belief that there's something wrong with her because she's been divorced twice.

3. Identify what energizes and drains you

Feeling guilty often has a lot to do with your energy level for certain activities. A wise professor of Shona's once told her that she identifies two kinds of activities in her life: those that energize her and those that drain her.[2] There are some things you do that make you come alive with energy and anticipation; other things completely drain you when you even think about them, and you'd give anything not to have to do them. That becomes a problem when it's something you're doing for your kids or your blended family as we often feel guilty because we believe we *should* like it, otherwise we're not good parents (there's that nasty should again).

The professor said she uses a quick but effective technique to figure out when she's doing something draining: she distinguishes between "have to's" and "want to's". For example, Shona does not really enjoy soccer all that much, but Ryan used to love it. She found that every time Ryan had a soccer game, she would hear herself saying to herself and other people, "I have to take Ryan to a soccer game tonight." The use of the words "have to" in your internal dialogue or external conversations is a pretty good indication you are resisting something in some way. You can use this simple identification technique to get a handle on things that are draining you, and either stop doing them ('cause you really don't want to anyway), or find some kind of understanding with yourself regarding how much you are willing to do and how you can make it work for you.

With regard to soccer, when Shona realized she was referring to it as a "have to," she knew she was resisting it; this made every soccer game a trial for her. A good way to reframe it is to begin to refer to these kinds of events as "I want to's." As soon as she began telling herself and others, "I want to go to Ryan's soccer game tonight," it freed her to concentrate on the real reason she went — to support and be interested in her son's activities.

Did it change her opinion and boredom with soccer? No, but at least she had a good understanding and made a clear choice that this was something she wanted to do for certain good reasons. It also allowed her to analyze the nature of her guilt. It went beyond merely not being interested in soccer; she felt like she had so many other things she'd rather be doing (pursuing her own interests, attending to household chores, etc.) than sitting on a soccer field for an hour and a half twice a week.

One thing Shona loves to do, but feels she hardly has any time for, is reading. So she started taking a book or the newspaper along with her to Ryan's soccer games. It's not that she read the entire time the game was on, and it's not that she didn't pay a lot of attention to the game (especially when Ryan was on the field). In fact, most of the time she got very little reading done at all. It's more that she had attended to her own psychological needs while at the same time keeping her son feeling happy and supported. Even the simple act of taking something along to read, should she feel the need, allowed her to relax and enjoy the soccer games more. Since then, Ryan has dropped out of soccer and does other things but it helped Shona get through it at the time.

Some parents may view that as selfish, feeling that you *should* be giving your undivided attention to your children at their events. The key point here, though, is that Shona found a way to be happy about doing something that she was previously singularly unhappy about and also met Ryan's need to have his mom there. It wasn't an option in her mind not to go — she just had to find a way to deal with it positively so it didn't feel like a drain on her life for which she felt guilty. In Chapter Eight, we're going to discuss the notion of enlightened selfishness as a key coping mechanism for surviving in a blended family.

Chapter Seven

Resistance is Futile

At fifteen life had taught me undeniably that surrender, in its place, was as honorable as resistance, especially if one had no choice.[1]

- Maya Angelou

A large part of the underlying success of blended families is the notion that Resistance is Futile. In other words, the more you resist the trials and tribulations that come your way, the more you are delaying the opportunity to get your blended family functioning happily and cohesively, and the more *you* contribute to problems that can result in a breakdown of the family. Frankly, it is simply not worth your energy to resist, argue about, debate, and otherwise stew over many of these issues or other conflicts. This merely diverts your energy from the task at hand, which is getting on with building a successful blended family.

Acceptance starts with an understanding on the part of both parents that the family will not be perfect. And we've just spent two chapters looking at numerous ways in which our families are not perfect. As we mentioned in Chapter One, many people have romantic notions about how happy and loving our blended families will be. It's a wonderful goal, and if you put a lot of effort into it, it's entirely possible you will get there. In the meantime, you have a number of hurdles to overcome. The reason we spent so much time talking about the strength of your marriage or partnership as part of the Recipe for Blended Family Success® is because that's where you need to start. Without that, the second ingredient, Acceptance, will not come easily to you —and as we've just learned in the previous chapter, there are many things you will need to accept.

Acceptance will always be your strongest defence against the stressors that will compete for your frustration daily. It will ensure your blood pressure stays low, and will allow you to think clearly, react reasonably, and engage fully in your blended family.

Okay, you're thinking, I understand the concept and it all sounds good, but how exactly do I do that? How do I let go of the things that are bothering me, gnawing at me, and just plain irritating me? Where do I start?

We have a favorite saying that goes, "Life is a ten-foot wall. Some people start at the bottom of the wall, some people start right on top, some people have to run fifty yards before they even reach the wall. But everyone has to get over that wall." Your blended family is part of your ten-foot wall. To live your life to its fullest and to be happy, you have to figure out how to get over that wall. Period. After all, what's the alternative?

Start with reality

The short version of explaining how to get over the wall is start with reality. There's no sense wasting your time wishing you didn't have all those challenges we've talked about, or that they're going to go away. They're not. Starting with reality means being completely honest with yourself about the challenges you face and any guilt feelings you have. Ideally, you and your partner could start by doing that together, but it's okay to do it alone first and then involve your partner.

One thing we learned early on was that it was okay to admit you didn't like one of the children that week. We all love our children, but depending on what life stage they're in and how challenging their behavior is, you definitely have days when you don't like them very much. And that's okay. Your children are entitled to go through difficult stages —in fact, it's expected. And the truth is you're not Mr. or Ms. Sunshine all the time either. But it feels somehow more acceptable to admit you do not like your biological child that week because you know there's an underlying and constant love for him or her at the same time. That's not necessarily true of your stepchildren. It can feel a little dangerous to admit to your partner —their parent —that you're just not that wild about his or her offspring right now. It's important to remember that it's temporary. Most of the time, your stepchildren will get over whatever it is that's driving you wild that week, and you'll return to more charitable feelings. This experience is true of any relationship we have in life, so take it easy on yourself when you feel that way about your stepchildren. Admit it to your partner as a way of venting your feelings. Laugh about it together. Reality is, they don't always like that same child either, even though he or she is theirs! When we started admitting that to each other, it became a lot easier to discuss issues and frustrations without taking offence.

Once you feel you have identified all the challenges and issues, identify the root cause behind every issue. Remember when we were analyzing our guilty feelings? We talked about asking why when trying to understand when you made a less than wonderful choice or decision. Here's how the technique called the Five Whys,' which we mentioned in the last chapter, can help you. You start by defining a challenge or issue and then ask why it is a problem —and you keep asking why until you finally get to the real reason, the root cause. It usually takes about five whys to finally figure out the root cause. It has been our experience that most first reactions to challenges and issues do not reflect the root cause. They are the symptoms of the problem, not the actual problem itself.

Here's an example. During the first year of our blended family relationship, we encountered many differences in our respective approaches to neatness, housework, and how we kept the house. Shona became frustrated at some habits exhibited by John and his children that left the house in what she considered a less than ideal state. In a moment of impatience over an untidy kitchen, she said to John, "You're not very good at cleaning up after yourself, are you?" Then she walked away to do something in another part of the house for a couple of hours. When she returned, she found John sitting quietly on the couch, looking serious. She knew something was up.

"I want to talk to you," said John. "It's about that comment you made about not cleaning up after myself. I'm offended by it and I've been trying to get to the root of why I'm feeling so bad." John had run himself through a Five Whys process that went something like this:

1. Why did that comment offend me so much? *Because it was an unkind thing to say.*

2. Why does it feel unkind? *Because I'm not trying to be messy. I really do my best to keep the house in a way all of us feel good about.*

3. Why is it important to me for Shona to acknowledge that I do try? *Because I don't want her to think badly of me.*

4. Why don't I want her to think badly of me? *Because our relationship is very, very important to me. It feels threatening to our relationship if she thinks badly of me.*

5. Why is it threatening to the relationship if Shona thinks badly of me? *Because then she might not love me anymore.*

At the root of his feelings and reaction was John's fear that his faults would mean Shona wouldn't love him anymore. It really wasn't about housework — it went much deeper than that. When John explained all of this to Shona, she understood why he was feeling so offended. While it was not her intention to offend him, and certainly not her intention to threaten the stability of the relationship, that's what she had done. John's willingness to be completely transparent about his thinking with Shona allowed both of us to remind ourselves of what's really important to us: our love for one another and its resulting kind regard.

The interesting thing about this situation is the deep-seated fear a seemingly minor comment brought out in John. On the surface, it was a throwaway comment. Underneath, and upon analysis, it got much more complicated than that. Shona has had similar reactions to comments John has made to her, and we have both found that using the Five Whys approach as a way to analyze our reactions is a powerful tool for helping us not only understand ourselves, but be completely transparent with each other. It is an incredibly powerful communication, conflict resolution, and relationship tool.

Free yourself from fear, reaction, and worry

If you look at the root cause of most of the blended family challenges and guilt issues we listed in the last chapter, you will see that the foundational feeling behind most of them is fear. Fear arises out of our need to have things go a certain way, to maintain the illusion that we have control (we don't!). When you can let go of your need to have things go a certain way —when you *accept* the way things *are* —you will experience a great sense of freedom not only in your blended family, but in all areas of your life.

The first thing Acceptance frees you from is fear; fear that there is something you won't have (a successful marriage, kids who are thrilled to be in a blended family, a good relationship with your stepchildren). Fear that there is something you have that you will lose (your partner, your kids' love, your kids). Fear that without things going a certain way, you won't be happy (your stepchildren liking you, your kids loving their new stepparent, your ex-partner falling off a tall building).

The next thing Acceptance frees you from is reaction. When you're not afraid of anything, you don't feel the need to defend, protect, criticize, or judge. This eliminates a heck of a lot of conflict and bad feeling that might potentially arise in your blended family.

By freeing you from fear and reaction, Acceptance allows you to become a much better listener and observer because you can hear and learn about others more effectively when you're not busy reacting. And because your attention is engaged in listening and observing, you are freed from a third thing: worry. Worrying is a completely useless drain on your energy because it tends to delay action. And the longer you delay action, the more you will worry because you will feel powerless to deal with the situation. Action tends to have the effect of increasing our sense of confidence thereby decreasing the amount of worry energy we put into things. You do yourself no good by worrying about what ifs —What if Rudie crashes the car? What if Ryan's behavior in fourth grade ruins his life? These are all passive, worry-oriented behaviors.

We once read a study about people having problems and feeling they needed a therapist to help them. They had spent a lot of time struggling through their problems, worried endlessly about them, and finally reached a decision to seek outside help. The funny thing was, the very act of making an appointment with a therapist got them moving on their problems. They actually took action simply as a result of making an appointment for help. Even more interesting was the fact that many potential patients no longer felt the need to attend a therapy session — they were on the road to solving it themselves. Action was no longer delayed and the necessary momentum for change was in place.

Because accepting the way things are helps to free you from fear, reaction, and worry, you are much better prepared to take the right action. For example, rather than worrying about Ryan's behavior in fourth grade, feeling fearful about it, and reacting, Acceptance allowed us to put some plans into place that helped Ryan modify his behavior. This kind of change doesn't happen overnight, but fourth-grade transgressions have rarely ruined anyone's life. In the case of worrying about a teenager crashing a car, getting injured or worse, there are just certain things in life we need to accept as part of the risk of being a parent. No amount of fear, worry, or even reaction is going to change the fact that life is inherently risky.

Shona remembers when Ryan first started daycare and went on a field trip in a school bus. She worried all day about the possibility of an accident (after all, buses don't have seat belts!) and called the daycare several times to see if the kids were back yet. After reflecting on how obsessive her behavior was, she realized she had to get the incessant worry about her child down to a dull roar in her mind or she was in for a fairly miserable life. It's true that all parents worry about their children, no matter how old they are, but you can't let it cripple your ability to allow them the freedom to learn how to make good choices.

When you get in the habit of practicing Acceptance rather than fear, reaction, and worry, you will have increasing glimpses into the peace of mind that true Acceptance can give you. It helps to practice on the small things before you graduate to the bigger ones.

Shona remembers a glimpse of Acceptance she experienced when the kids were smaller. It was a relatively minor incident but a useful lesson nonetheless in "non-reaction." She was rushing around one morning, busily trying to get Ryan and Kate off to school and daycare and herself off to work. Everything was going really well, everyone was dressed and ready to go, and for once, she was going to get out the door a little early! She was feeling really good and ready to get to work to dive into an interesting new project. Of course, that's exactly when "the incident" happened.

When Shona called Kate to get her shoes on, Kate came running out of the kitchen with a full glass of cranberry juice (she had helped herself to more without Shona's knowledge), promptly spilling it all over the living room carpet. Have we mentioned that our carpet is light beige? There was a huge, bright, now-soaking-in puddle of cranberry juice right smack in the middle of the living room, not to mention hundreds of spots scattered across the rest of the carpet and on the surrounding walls.

For a moment time seemed to stop. Kate stood with a look of horror on her face, staring at Mom, waiting for the onslaught. Shona stood frozen on the spot, a million reactions flying through her head ranging from disappointment at being late again to homicidal intent aimed at her youngest. Ryan stood watching, his mouth hanging open with a slight hint of glee in his eyes stemming from gratitude that he was not the perpetrator of this heinous crime —and evil satisfaction that his sister was.

The paralysis was broken with a gut-wrenching wail from Kate. Ryan smugly offered to stay home from school and clean up. Shona declined, and as she tried to comfort Kate and get her to stop screaming, a wonderful thing happened. A strange kind of calm came over her. In that moment, she accepted that all of her carefully laid plans for getting to work early were now out the window. There was nothing to do but pull out the steam cleaner and get working on the carpet. She briefly considered throwing caution to the wind and just leaving, but after reflecting on how bad it would be to deal with a *dried* cranberry juice stain after work, she gave herself up to the inevitable. She recalls it being an absolutely marvellous feeling. It took her a full hour to steam clean the big spot plus attend to all of the tiny spots on the rest of the carpet and wall (with Kate happily watching cartoons in the bedroom), but the feeling of calmness lasted all day.

Shona wishes she could bottle that feeling every time some minor irritation occurs because then she'd be serene all the time! More importantly, if we can learn to practice Acceptance in such small situations, it helps us build capacity to practice Acceptance in much more serious ones. Again, that's easier said than done. To make it easier, we've identified (based on hard-won experience) ten approaches you can take to bring more Acceptance into your everyday blended family life. Read on to discover what they are.

Chapter Eight

The Ten Laws of Acceptance

Acceptance is not submission; it is acknowledgement of the facts of a situation, then deciding what you're going to do about it.[1]

  - Kathleen Casey Theisen

It's all very well to say that resistance is futile and that you need to free yourself from fear, reaction, and worry. But you actually have to do more than think it —you have to live it. It's got to be something you take practical steps toward.

That's where the *Ten Laws of Acceptance* come in. These are ten things we've learned can help you live the philosophy of Acceptance in your blended family:

1. Understand that you can change only yourself

2. Notice where you're existing

3. Beware of frozen judgments

4. Embrace your dark side

5. Commit to transparency

6. Force self-reflection

7. Practice enlightened selfishness

8. Admit when you're wrong

9. Pick the right hill to die on

10. Make the first move.

Let's take a look at what these laws look like in practice.

Law #1: Understand that you can change only yourself

One of the true paradoxes of life is that the more we try to change people, the more they will resist our efforts to change them. It doesn't really matter if they think the change is good or not, just the very fact that we're trying to convince them it's good for them will virtually guarantee they will toss your suggestions on their floor like yesterday's dirty laundry. It's as sure as death and taxes. Equally as sure is the fact that good intentions followed by good modeling, all performed consistently, will allow others to make choices for themselves about the changes they will (willingly) make.

Some people are quite anxious about potty training their children, like somehow there is a magic age by which everyone *must* cast off their pull-ups. Or what? The diaper police will swoop down upon your house and carry you all off to jail? We're here to tell you that we have yet to meet a fully functioning adult who isn't potty trained.

The simple message? People (children or adults) will make decisions for themselves about the changes they wish to make. No amount of your trying to convince them will have an effect. In fact, you will probably only create conflict and resistance, both of which again are guaranteed to result in no change in behavior.

Shona's experience with potty training Ryan is a great example of this. He was approaching the age of three very quickly with no apparent sign in sight that diapers would be a thing of the past. Shona tried convincing him, bribing him with rewards, telling him how big boys used the toilet, but nothing worked. It wasn't that he didn't know when he needed to go to the toilet. It wasn't like he didn't know how to use the toilet. He had clearly demonstrated on numerous occasions that he knew how to do both. He simply hadn't yet made an inner decision that he was willing to use the toilet. In the end, it was nothing Shona did that caused him to use the toilet —it was the friends he met at daycare. The moment he realized that all the girls and the vast majority of the boys at his daycare were already potty trained, he decided there would be no more diapers for him. He came home that day, announced the fact to Shona, and from that moment forward never wore another diaper or pull-up and never had an accident.

How many parents tell their kids they won't get a good job unless they work hard in school? And how many kids actually respond with, "Oh, yes, Mother and Father, you are absolutely right. I'll go and do my homework this minute instead of going to a movie." We're willing to bet the answer is zero, but if it's worked for you, please let the Guinness Book of World Records know as it's definitely one for the record books.

So, if you can't convince others to change, where does that leave you? It leaves you with your own behavior through modeling. It leaves you with attending to your own reactions. The only thing you can change about your interactions with others is you because it's the only thing you have direct control over. Acceptance goes a long way in helping you train yourself to do that. Every time you feel yourself getting irritated or reactive, stop. In every circumstance, ask yourself "What would Acceptance look like? Is this something I need to work on accepting? What boundaries can I set so that I don't keep getting irritated?"

One example is Shona's frustration with one of the older children's perennial forgetfulness. Most of the time when she leaves a message on his answering machine, he forgets to return it. He forgets commitments he's made to baby sit, come for coffee, or meet people at restaurants. The biggest forgetful incident was when he made a commitment to stay at the house for a week with the younger children so we could take advantage of a trip to Mexico we had won. He forgot. We didn't go to Mexico.

Shona was getting quite upset and got stuck in a repeating cycle of trying again, getting upset when the behavior didn't change, and then doing it all over again. She decided she didn't want to continue to be irritated all the time because she genuinely likes him, and she realized that she was choosing to put herself in situations that would create exactly that reaction. When she came to that realization, she decided from that moment on she would no longer have any expectation that this child would remember appointments. She doesn't ask him to baby sit, or if John asks him to, she accepts that he may not show up. Ditto for coffee appointments, lunch dates, and family gatherings. This attitude has freed her up to simply enjoy her stepson when he does show up, and not be irritated about it when he doesn't. It's really all about managing our own expectations of people.

Does Shona still think that her stepson needs to get better organized and live up to his commitments? Absolutely. But no amount of suggestion, cajoling, and irritation has changed his behavior. In the end, all you can do is change your own reaction to the behavior. Sooner or later, reactions from the outside world to this forgetfulness will cause him to make an inner decision to change. Until then, all we can do is create our own boundaries and accept. We'll talk about boundaries in more detail in Chapter Eleven.

Law #2: Notice where you're existing

Notice where you're *existing* in your mind. In other words, where are you focusing your energy in your internal conflicts and thoughts? Are you constantly reliving the day your stepson lied to you about where he was and are therefore unable to forgive and trust him, or are you living day to day with the understanding that all people change and he was genuinely sorry for having lied to you that time? Holding grudges is harmful to *your* mental health, not the mental health of the person who has wronged you. It's also not helpful in resolving conflict.

Take a look at where you are existing: in the time that he lied to you, or in the time that he cleaned the kitchen without your asking? Our behavior is a product of our inner thoughts, and it is a sad fact of the human condition that we generally get what we expect (positive or negative). What you focus on, you get. Give your stepchildren a chance to surprise you and look for the good. Choose to exist in those places instead of the places where they disappointed you.

Law #3: Beware of frozen judgments

What we mean by this is the tendency of humans to decide that people are a certain way and despite evidence to the contrary continue to hold that belief. In other words, their judgments become frozen. For example, one thing that drives Shona nuts about her family of origin is that they believe she is a very messy person. When she was a teenager living at home, she would often toss her belongings into a closet after her mother had told her to clean her room. She had wanted to do it quickly so she could go back to whatever it was she had been doing in the first place. Her mother would come by and be satisfied the room was clean, but would later open the closet and everything would tumble out on top of her.

To this day everyone tells stories about Shona's messy closet and continues to think of her in that way. This obviously doesn't give any credit for growth and maturation, and when she has asked them to please reframe their comments and opinions in this regard in light of how well she generally keeps our house, they continue to make fun of it. Never forget that each of us is a work in progress, and that at any given time, people will be growing, changing, evolving. We show people little respect when we insist on living on past impressions of them.

An extension of this is when people become upset because another person has changed his or her mind. One powerful speech Shona recently heard was about how each of us, at any time, has the right to change our mind. As you've already learned, Shona struggled with guilty feelings for years over being divorced twice. In fact, she was so ashamed of it that when she first met John, she was scared to tell him about it lest he think less of her for it. When she did tell him, he saw it only as an indication of courage — that she found herself in situations that were untenable for her and took action. Sometimes that action was clumsy and could have been handled better, but nevertheless he complimented her for being willing to make changes for her own happiness.

This was quite a revelation to Shona, for never once had anyone framed her so-called marital failures in such a growth-oriented way. John's reaction, coupled with hearing that speech about having a right to change your mind, has allowed her to free herself from guilt at failing or not being good at relationships to feeling like she had the courage to change her mind.

This is a powerful freedom to grant anyone, including your children. Life never stays the same, and if this week your stepchild doesn't like you and next week he does, that's okay. He has a right to change his mind. After all, all of us are constantly trying roles and feelings on for size to see how they fit us. Children are just much more overt about it.

Law #4: Embrace your dark side

Accept the dark side of yourself. One of Shona's good friends, Sandi, always makes Shona confess any petty thoughts she might have in certain situations. Her belief is that if you get them on the table, you've vented them and they're gone. And it's often true. We do the same thing with each other.

No matter how nice you are, no matter how good a person you try to be, there will always be petty little thoughts and feelings that creep up on you that you would rather not admit to. Embrace them, don't ignore them. They are wonderful hints about all the shoulds you put on yourself.

If you find yourself thinking your teenage stepdaughter is loose for wearing skimpy clothes, embrace and explore the feeling. What is really at the core of it? Is it because you're jealous that you don't have that young, flawless body anymore (or maybe you never did) and you secretly wish that you could wear those clothes and look good in them too?

Do you find yourself wishing your wife hadn't lost all that weight and wanting her to go back to eating tubs of ice cream with you at night again so you won't feel so bad about that beer belly you need to lose?

Do you find yourself constantly annoyed at your stepson who repeatedly asks you why when you want him to do something, when you know very well that you don't have a good reason for it and can't defend your point of view?

Celebrate your little evil thoughts. Embrace them. They are wonderful opportunities to explore just why something is getting under your skin. We bet that 99 times out of a 100, you'll discover it's something to do with you, not what the other person is doing. Whatever the situation, by venting or exploring your uncharitable thoughts, you will have dealt with them and let them go.

Law #5: Commit to transparency

Live by the *Law of Transparency* in your blended family. What this means is in all cases (and age-appropriately of course) explain your thinking, your reasoning, your assumptions, your feelings. Leave nothing out and be completely open and honest. Most importantly, do not offer judgment of others' behavior, simply observation. Not only will people gain a better understanding of what's going on in your head (often they see only your reactions), but everyone can remain more objective and non-reactive because they know what people's motivations are.

We have had many discussions in our family about the notion of intention we mentioned earlier: when someone does or says something hurtful or annoying, instead of reacting to the comment or action, try to think about the intention behind the action or comment. Most of the time, the intention is a good one or it reveals a sincere need the other person has. For example, if you feel like your stepchildren are always attacking you, look for the reason behind it. An attack is often a call for help. What do they need help with? Are they missing their mother? Wanting to spend more time with their father? Wanting more attention from you? Take some time to reflect on the intention behind the behavior, and you will invariably get a different view of the person and the situation. When you've gained that understanding, you can feel a lot more comfortable about being transparent about your own intentions.

Law #6: Force self-reflection

When we talked about the Five Whys techniques, we were addressing the concept of self-reflection in ourselves as parents. But there's real value in also requiring your children to self-reflect. The Five Whys approach may not work for them as their brains are not fully developed in terms of abstract thinking, but there is something practical you can do to get them to think about their behavior, especially when you're furious with them.

One approach we find works particularly well is restraining ourselves from immediately imposing a punishment; instead, we force the children to reflect. One memorable event involved then seventeen-year-old Rudie staying out all night with a girlfriend and two male friends when she told us that she was staying overnight at another girlfriend's. We would have been none the wiser if it weren't for the fact that the mother of the girlfriend she was with showed up at our house at eight a.m. on a Sunday morning looking for the girls. When Rudie finally showed up around noon and we inquired if she had a good time at her sleepover, the real story (or at least as much as she was willing to tell us) emerged. It seems they had decided to go into the nearest city and drive around. Finally getting bored, the four of them rented a hotel room to watch movies and eat pizza. We asked Rudie why she couldn't have just done that at home. She agreed sheepishly, and said that to add insult to injury, she now owed her share of the cost of the hotel room and the pizza, something she could ill-afford as she was saving up to go to Mexico.

Her girlfriend was immediately grounded for three weeks, which promptly sparked a round of scheming about how to get around it, sneak out of house, etc. She had something to push against with her parents, and by God she was going to do it. Additionally, now her activities went completely underground and her parents had no clue as to what was going on in her life and with her friends. We're not sure what happened to the boys. As for Rudie, after the confession came out, she inquired what her father was going to do to punish her. He said he didn't know and wanted to think about it before saying the worst words of all, "I trusted you and I'm very disappointed in you." She glumly descended to her room to await her fate.

One day went by...two days went by...three days. No decision on punishment from her dad. In the meantime, Rudie was clearly wracked by remorse, looked miserable, and was doing everything she could to make up for it, such as cleaning the house before we got home from work, preparing dinner and ensuring the kitchen was spotless, offering to look after the baby, even cleaning the bathroom! Shona watched all of this with interest and finally asked John on the fourth day if he had decided what he was going to do. He laughed and replied, "Nothing. She's punishing herself enough! I think the lesson is learned. Why rub it in with useless stuff like grounding, which will just make her resentful and rebellious? We have a lot more moral high ground by being fair rather than punitive."

By the end of the fifth day, Rudie could stand it no more and finally blurted out after dinner, "Okay, get it over with. Tell me what my punishment is!" John merely quietly replied, "Well, I think you've tortured yourself sufficiently to get the point. I now consider it over." She blinked in surprise and immediately called her friends to kibitz about how her dad had handled it maturely.

In the years since then, we have come to suspect that there was much more to the story than we were told, but in the end, it doesn't really matter. Rudie experienced a great deal of remorse over *whatever* happened that night and for lying to us, and isn't your goal with teenagers ultimately to influence them to be honest, responsible people who make good choices? We are confident that that incident, whatever parts of it we were never privy to, at least taught Rudie a small lesson in self-reflection, honesty, and good choices. Realistically, you probably can't teach them all that in one lesson and often just need to be happy with the small lessons that accumulate along the way. In the end, a complete character emerges: a kind, thoughtful, increasingly responsible young woman who is a pleasure to be around and of whom you can be very proud.

Law #7: Practice enlightened selfishness

Many years ago, Shona was sitting in a cancer clinic awaiting treatment. Anyone with a serious illness knows that waiting rooms are often the most negative part of your experience — the anticipation can be worse than the cure. Across from her sat a gaunt and tired-looking man. Distraction is often the best way to deflect the all-consuming fear filling an idle patient's mind, so she started a conversation with him.

It turns out he wasn't a cancer patient — his wife was. And she had a particularly rare form of cancer for which there was no cure. Shona felt inadequate to the conversation as her own illness was of the early-detection-equals-cure variety. She had to endure only a few more treatments and then proceed happily with her life.

This man had depleted his life savings traveling the world to find a cure. They had tried every treatment known to man and a few he had invented on his own. Shona commented on how devoted he was to his wife, selflessly giving up work and friends in support of finding her deliverance.

He stared at her silently for a moment. "It looks like I've done all this for my wife. And I have," he said. "But the truth is I've done this mostly for myself. I can't live without her. Searching the world for a cure is the *most* selfish thing I've ever done."

There are certain events in life that cause us to completely reframe how we view things. In that moment, the man's description of his selfishness had that effect on Shona. Why do we view this thing called selfishness so negatively? Certainly he was helping his wife as well as helping himself. That was good, wasn't it?

Later, Shona discovered the word "selfish" is a relatively new one. Scholars' best guess is that it arose about 360 years ago due to the Protestant religious movement. Prior to that, the expression most commonly used was self-love. To this day, most dictionaries note self-love as a synonym for selfishness.

Most of us will agree there's a big difference between self-love and selfishness. You might argue that selfishness is about doing things for yourself that may cause inconvenience or pain for others, while self-love is healthy self-regard that doesn't inconvenience or pain others.

The truth is, though, sometimes self-love *does* inconvenience or pain others, despite our best intentions. So it appears that the distinguishing element between the two words is *intention* — do we intend to do harm or are we doing our best to honor ourselves without hurting others? In the final analysis, selfishness can actually mean healthy self-regard — as long as our intentions are good. This is what we call enlightened selfishness.

After her conversation with the man in the cancer clinic, the concept of enlightened selfishness became an important one for Shona. Up to that point, she had lived her life believing she didn't have the right to say no to others, even if she wanted to.

Enlightened selfishness can be a struggle for men, yet women tend to experience it more often because they're taught to be nurturing and giving. Saying no is not what nice girls do, so we say yes first and figure out how to deliver on our promise later. Heaven forbid we turn down a request — we might be accused of being selfish.

The concept of personal boundaries is closely related to that of enlightened selfishness. Boundaries are internal lines you will not allow others to cross. These are values-based thoughts and feelings about what is important to you and when you should say yes or no. We'll get into dealing with boundaries in more detail in Chapter Eleven.

The inability to practice enlightened selfishness can lead to a variety of troubling situations, some fairly inconsequential, some life changing. If we can't say no in less serious situations, we don't have the skills to say no in more critical situations, such as relationships, career, health.

Many stress-related issues are related to how much we're willing to say no to others' demands. Whether it's work or personal, the more you tolerate, the more people demand. If we teach people we'll drop everything the minute they need us, they'll expect us to do it every time. If we take on more work than we can reasonably handle —and pull it off anyway —our reward is more work.

While selfishness is not a term that enjoys particularly positive connotations in our society, we're suggesting that you actually do yourself a disservice, especially in navigating all the demands of a blended family, when you don't set some healthy boundaries for yourself. This appears to be particularly challenging for women who will much more readily give up their own needs and desires in favor of their children, stepchildren, and spouse. It's a slippery slope, though, because the practice of always putting your own needs last can, and usually does, lead to resentment.

Unfortunately, it's a completely unnecessary resentment because it's totally within the control of the individual making the concessions. John observed Shona doing this a lot with all the children over everything from what movie to watch to who got to have the last piece of chocolate cake. He has taught her it is okay sometimes to say, "No, children, I am going to have the last piece of cake because I want it." The reality is that if you don't learn how to assert even these simple wishes for yourself, you end up getting your boundaries violated in a whole range of infinitely more important ways, ways that can have a very negative effect on your partnership and your blended family.

Law #8: Admit when you're wrong

As we mentioned earlier, research indicates that the largest, most powerful, single thing you can do to build and enhance your children's self-esteem is admitting when you're wrong. Admitting you're wrong applies equally to your dealings with your children and stepchildren as it does to dealings with your partner. With your younger kids, admitting you're wrong lets them know that no one is perfect and also builds their self-esteem; they learn it's okay to make mistakes *and* admit to them.

It's the same with teenagers. One of the prime reasons for conflict between any kind of parent and teenagers is that they often feel trapped, judged, watched, and misunderstood. When parents are willing to work on themselves and admit errors (I made a mistake there, I wasn't the perfect dad, etc), it's amazing to see the harmony that can be achieved within the family. When you react this way, you are not giving your children anything to push against, so you eliminate conflict. That opens the door for genuine transparency and dialogue.

Law #9: Pick the right hills to die on

Lest you think we are advocating a letting go philosophy of child rearing, allow us to expand. There are times when, no matter how much you try to achieve understanding, your kids will resist you and you must simply put your foot down. We don't mean to create the impression that as long as you take these wonderful Acceptance measures with yourself and attempt to address all of your children's concerns fairly that everything will be great all the time. It won't. You are, after all, the parents, and however much you want to create democratic conditions, reality is you aren't living in a democracy; rather, you're living in a situation where younger people are looking to you for guidance and direction. You are the leaders, and not only does that mean the buck stops with you, you are also responsible for creating rules and ensuring everyone abides by them.

Despite the fact you will need to put your foot down, it's important that you engage in strategic approaches. Ask yourself if this is an issue that's really worth a pitched battle, or can you let it go with a few comments? Being strategic about the battles in which you engage wins you credibility with your children and stepchildren alike. In other words, you need to pick the right hills to die on.

A good way to figure out which are the right hills is to ask yourself the questions, "Is this going to matter one year from now? How about in five years? What about ten?" Many times, just going through this exercise can give you a much clearer perspective on the battles to fight and the battles in which you will lay down your arms. Along with this goes the understanding and acceptance that sometimes there are no good solutions and there are no happy endings.

Shona remembers a time when Ryan was four and they were visiting her parents. Ryan loved to cut out pictures from catalogues and drawings he had done, and he was dropping a lot of small bits of paper on his grandmother's carpet. Shona's mother was getting distressed by it until Shona pointed out to her that it was just paper —it wouldn't mark the rug, it was fairly easy and quick to clean up, and Ryan was having a lot of fun being creative. Would this issue really matter an hour from now? Her mom realized all of those things were true, and that she was getting too hung up on keeping her house neat rather than enjoying Ryan's creativity.

Of course you will encounter many more serious issues with your children that go well beyond dropping bits of paper on the floor. Personal safety, peer interactions, issues around drugs and alcohol, etc. are often tougher to navigate because the consequences of not addressing them can be tragic. There certainly isn't as much ambiguity around whether or not these are hills to die on because most of the time they are. We urge to you reflect, however, on whether you're dealing with isolated incidents or behaviors that are now trends. Many of the more serious issues are entirely normal stages of development and independence assertion, despite their potentially drastic outcomes. Again, as in most things, be as transparent as possible with your children regarding not only your concerns, but the reasoning behind the disciplinary measures you choose to employ. They won't like those reasons, but they can respect them if they understand then.

Law #10: Make the first move

Be the one to make the first move, even if you're the wronged party. Don't wait for the others to start. Somebody has to start. Let that somebody be you. The reality is that many wars and conflicts in our world could be averted if people would just stop adding up the who did what tally, put it aside, and make a fresh start. Besides, it is often very difficult to decide who was wrong and who was right, for most people define wrong as what is different from them.

One thing we always say to our children is that in life, if you are ever faced with the prospect of being right or being kind, choose kind every time. Being right will probably win you the battle, but it will also almost certainly guarantee you will lose the war. For example, you can argue and win a battle with your stepchild over the way he needs to keep his room, but you may well lose your ultimate goal in this war —to build an amicable, peaceful, and happy relationship with him and your entire blended family. Is a tidy room really that important?

Again, you need to consider the age of the child when deciding who needs to make the first move. With teenagers, it may well be a conscious decision on your part to wait and see what they do in terms of making a move to resolve a conflict with you. They are entirely capable of handling this kind of abstract behavior and thinking, although younger children aren't. If you mess up with a younger child, the sooner you make the first move to resolve it, the sooner they will learn that you are firm but fair, and, again, that you're not perfect.

When all else fails, use patience as a replacement for Acceptance until you can genuinely feel Acceptance or deal with the issue. There are some things that are just going to take time to be worked out, and there are some things that will never be worked out.

In the first instance, while you may not be willing to accept a certain situation in the long run, you can tolerate it in the short run because you know the timing is not right. An example of this latter point is John's discipline role in Ryan's life. At the beginning of our blended family, there were some things that John did not care for about Ryan's behavior. However, he was also aware that he needed time to ease into the role of parent/disciplinarian or he might well irreparably damage his long-term relationship with Ryan and potentially with Shona. He made a conscious decision that he would defer acting on those issues until the family and his relationship with Ryan were more firmly established.

In the second instance, sometimes you need to exercise patience to buy yourself time to realize you can't *ever* solve it. One blended family we know struggles with the differing interests and personalities of the father and his stepson. The father is a sports fanatic, living for every football and basketball game that's on TV or down at the local community center. His stepson has no interest in sports whatsoever and most of the time can be found with his nose buried deep in a book or researching some obscure scientific fact (he's twelve-years-old). Many times, the father has dragged his stepson off to a game, thinking that exposure will create interest. Not so. In fact, the more the father forces his stepson to accompany him to sports events, the more the stepson resents him.

This is one situation where their interests are never going to coincide and there's absolutely nothing wrong with that. The main issue is with the father, not the stepson. Having no sons of his own, he developed an expectation (or maybe even a dream) that he and his new stepson would share a love of sports and it would give them something to bond over. Reality is, it's never going to happen. The father needs to accept this and stop trying to force the issue. His energy would be much better spend identifying and acting on things they do have in common. Both of them love movies, for example. Perhaps they could establish a regular father-and-stepson movie night where Mom and the sisters aren't invited.

Exercising patience can buy you valuable time to learn and observe, to give you a more complete picture than was initially evident. In fact, impatience often signals your own resistance to learning, something that will not serve your interests or the interests of the blended family in the long run. Pay attention to where you are impatient, and use the skills of analysis we've talked about to help you figure out where it's coming from. You may be quite justified in your impatience, but is it truly resolving anything?

Part 4

Ingredient #3: Communication

The single biggest problem in communication is the illusion that it has taken place.[1]

- George Bernard Shaw

Chapter Nine

Managing Alien Communication

Feelings of worth can flourish only in an atmosphere where individual differences are appreciated, mistakes are tolerated, communication is open, and rules are flexible — the kind of atmosphere that is found in a nurturing family.[1]
    - Virginia Satir

The third ingredient in the Recipe for Blended Family Success® is Communication. As this is such a huge and complicated topic, we will spend the next four chapters highlighting some key challenges and tools to address them.

There's an old saying that the definition of insanity is doing the same thing you've always done over and over again and expecting the same result. If that's true, then we think most of us are teetering on the brink of being committed.

It constantly amazes us how many people seem to believe that talking more, asking more, yelling more loudly will actually change someone's behavior. Worse, the more you talk, ask, and yell, the more you are training the other person (be it spouse or child) to tune you out. That's your cue to try a different approach.

One area in which we never seem to learn our lesson about changing the way we do things is in male-female communication. Even though we've all heard of various books telling us that men and women are from different planets, we seem to forget, or at least not put into effect, the lessons others teach us about how men and women respond differently to the same situation. Continuing to do the same thing in your couple relationship that hasn't worked so far isn't all of a sudden miraculously going to work now. In fact, it will make it even more difficult to figure out how you can jointly develop a family vision both of you can live with. To make sense of this complicated thing called male/female communication, let's examine the different ways men and women approach the world. We'll use that as our starting point for creating brand new ways to communicate in your blended family.

Deborah Tannen, a linguistics professor at Georgetown University in Washington, is one of the leading experts on the differences between male and female communication. She is careful to point out that male and female styles of conversation are equally valid and, contrary to what many of us perceive, men are not trying to dominate women and women are not trying to manipulate men. There are simply feminine and masculine styles of discourse. Following along the lines of some of her key findings, below are some examples of how we see these gender-based communication styles creating challenges in our blended family.[2]

Contests vs. cooperation

Men grow up in a world in which a conversation is often a contest, either to achieve the upper hand or to prevent people from pushing them around. For women, however, talking is often a way to exchange confirmation and support.

This difference probably accounts for why John will sometimes take offence at something Ryan says whereas Shona doesn't see what's so offensive about it. For example, recently during an extremely busy and tiring weekend when we were working hard on home renovations, we ended up purchasing fast food for both lunch and dinner on the same day. It wasn't ideal and rarely occurs, but it was all we could cope with that day. When Ryan entered the dining room at dinnertime to see a second meal that was not home cooked, he said, "Perhaps tomorrow we could eat some healthier food." His facial expression and body language communicated disgust and negativity. John immediately lost it, barking at Ryan that he should appreciate what he was given and be thankful. You know —a variation on "think of all the starving kids in India" line.

Shona, while irritated at Ryan's unthinking comment, was also simultaneously pleased that Ryan had obviously observed the lessons of healthy eating we had been trying to teach. In fact, she wanted to compliment and support him on his mature approach to thinking about food for such a young boy.

John's perspective? Ryan's comment really meant, "You're too lazy to cook food for us," which was particularly offensive, seeing as we had both worked so hard all day. He also interpreted it to mean, "This is not good enough," and saw it as a challenge to his role of family chef.

While Shona admitted Ryan could have handled the situation better, she was also somewhat mystified at the vehemence of John's reaction. While John saw it as a challenge to gain the upper hand, Shona saw it as a confirmation that Ryan had taken in some important lessons about healthy eating and wanted to support it.

Separateness vs. closeness

Since women often think in terms of closeness and support they struggle to preserve intimacy. Men, concerned with status, tend to focus more on independence. These traits can lead women and men to have starkly different views of the same situation.

Struggles that highlight the differences between a focus on separateness and closeness in communication don't present too many issues for us as couple. However, Shona recalls an incident with her first husband when he made a commitment with friends for them to go camping over a long holiday weekend a few months away. When he announced the plans to Shona, she was upset —not so much about the camping plans, but because he hadn't talked to her about it first.

"But we've always gone camping on this particular holiday weekend," he explained. "I know that," Shona replied, "but why didn't you tell them you had to make sure it was okay with me first? Perhaps I had other ideas either for me or for both of us."

"I can't tell my friends that I have to ask my wife for permission!" he indignantly responded. Shona replied that it wasn't about permission, it was about consideration. Her ex-husband felt that to check with her usurped his independence. It made him feel like a child or somehow inferior. Shona was only too happy to check with him regarding social plans because she felt it showed their closeness to the rest of the world.

While the issue of separateness versus closeness doesn't come up too much between us, it does come up between Shona and Ryan. He recently asked Shona if it was okay if he brought some friends home after school to play video games. She told him that, on days on which he wanted to bring kids homes, he could call her from school to check if that day was good. He looked decidedly uncomfortable. When she asked him about his look, he explained that he didn't want his friends to think that he had to check with Mom every time he wanted some kids over. Shona explained that it was more a function of what days she needed Ryan to be home after school to look after Kate, that it was about consideration and family responsibilities, not permission. While Ryan understood that, he didn't want to be put in a position of checking with Mom in front of his friends.

Part of that is just normal teenage interaction with parents. It's not cool to be seen talking to your mom on the street, never mind phoning her for permission to have a friend over. But part of it is also a male tendency to appear independent in interactions, even if there is a distinct interdependency.

Solutions vs. empathy

To men, a complaint or a problem is a challenge to come up with a solution. But often women are simply looking for emotional support, not a solution. They already know what to do.

When Shona comes home and starts talking to John about a situation at work or with a friend, John has learned to ask early in the conversation, "Do you want help solving the problem or do you just want to vent?" Most of the time, she just wants to vent, but sometimes she wants help solving the problem. However, until we established this system of identifying the goal of the conversation, John would often go immediately into problem-solving mode. The result? Shona would feel offended because she knew perfectly well how to solve the problem — she just wanted to explore her feelings and reactions about it first.

Men are not consciously trying to take over when they go into problem solving mode. They're just being action-oriented and providing advice they believe to be helpful. Women, on the other hand, are merely looking for a sympathetic ear to air their grievances with and have no requirement for their listener to solve their problems unless they specifically ask for it.

Facts vs. feelings

We see and hear it in the media all the time — women get hurt when men don't talk to them, but many men are frustrated when they disappoint their partners and don't know why. What is vital to understand is that by and large, society trains men to keep their innermost thoughts to themselves and generally use conversation as a way to exchange facts. Women get a lot more practice in and support for verbalizing their feelings as they grow up. Indeed, Tannen's studies show that they talk a lot more in private conversations than men do.[3]

With our friends and even in our own past relationships, we have observed that often, when a couple breaks up, the man says the fact that his wife wants a divorce comes as a big shock to him, that he never knew she was so unhappy. On the other hand, the wife says she's talked to him endlessly about her feelings and their problems and he never did anything to solve them, and she is genuinely confused as to why he didn't understand that their marriage was in trouble.

The men were hearing a lot of talk about feelings, but because they are oriented toward facts, they didn't hear the underlying message: we're headed for divorce if we don't solve these problems. Women tend to communicate information using their feelings to illustrate the underlying message. Generally, other women will get their message, but often men do not.

One of the things that used to constantly amuse us in our house was our individual reactions to our workdays. When Shona used to work with ninety-five percent men, she would frequently come home desperate for conversation and connection considering that she rarely had any dialogue during the day where she felt she had connected with her colleagues' real feelings; she often described her work environment as sterile. John, who worked with ninety-five percent women, often came home desperate for peace and quiet because he'd talked with everyone all day about feelings; he often described his work environment as draining and emotionally exhausting. It was a stark (and somewhat amusing) example of the facts versus feelings dichotomy in male/female communications.

Requirements vs. requests

Women tend to try to win agreement to get people to do what they want. Remember, they are oriented toward empathy and connection. Men will be much more direct, and sometimes can feel manipulated and respond more resentfully when they're being asked indirectly than they would to a straightforward request.

John often observes Shona trying to suggest, convince, or cajole the children into doing (or not doing something): "Wouldn't it be better if you used your crayons on the table instead of the carpet?" "You may want to consider getting a part-time job during the school year." "Perhaps buying a motorcycle will delay your plans to travel to Australia." Often, because her requirements are phrased as requests, she will get drawn into negotiations with the children without even realizing it. "How about I just color one picture here and then move to the table?"

"I'm not sure part-time work fits with my desired lifestyle." "But I want a motorcycle *and* a trip to Australia." John will simply put his foot down, firmly and directly: "Put your crayons on the table and color there." "You're going to need a part-time job to cover the bills this year." "You have to decide which you want more —a motorcycle or a trip to Australia."

One night, Shona asked Ryan to take out the garbage. Or she thought she did. What she actually said was, "Ryan, do you think you could take out the garbage?" He looked thoughtful for a moment and then replied, "No, I'm doing something else right now." Shona barked at Ryan, "It's not a choice, Ryan. I'm telling you to take out the garbage. Now." Poor Ryan was confused. He thought Mom had given him a choice by the way she had phrased her request. He heard it as something he was free to accept or reject. Shona has had to learn how to be very direct in her requests of Ryan.

On the other hand, when Shona wants Kate to do something, she finds she can use her usual communication style. Kate hears "Do you think you can clean up your toys now?" as a direct request to pick up her toys at that moment.

Confrontation vs. negotiation

In trying to prevent fights, women will often refuse to openly oppose the will of others. Men will much more often engage in open conflict because they are trained to not let anyone get one up on them.

One memorable conflict Shona had with her second husband was over what to name their son. Months before he was born, Shona said, "I've always liked the name Collin. I'd like to call the baby that if it's a boy." Her husband mumbled something about the name being okay, and Shona took that as agreement.

When the baby was born, Shona confidently commented that she was so happy his name would be Collin. Her ex-husband balked. "I never agreed to name him Collin," he protested. "Yes you did!" Shona replied. He refused to relent, and the conflict remained unresolved for three days while the baby continued nameless. Shona didn't openly argue with her husband during that time because it seemed like such a petty argument in the face of what was supposed to be a joyous event, but it festered in her mind.

As she was in the hospital for five days following the baby's birth, she ended up being alone when the hospital staff brought the official paperwork to register the baby's name and birth. She admits that she strongly considered just registering the baby's name as Collin and be done with it. In the end, she decided that that would be much too manipulative and not compromise oriented, so she ended up registering the baby's name as the one name both she and her husband said they could live with: Ryan.

Because she had made that compromise, she then expected her husband would be willing to compromise on Ryan's middle name. After all, negotiation is all about trying to have both sides get a little of what they want and also give up a little. Not so. He wanted Ryan to have his name as a middle name, and Shona wanted him to have a family name that had been passed down for generations on her side. Because there was very little difference between the two names (her husband's name was Michael and her family name was Carmichael), she felt it was yet another good compromise. Her husband refused, Shona furiously gave in out of sheer frustration, and Ryan's middle name is Michael. Unfortunately, to this day Shona still carries some resentment over the issue, first, because she was mad at herself for giving in, and second, because she was mad at her ex-husband for being so unmoveable. He had seemed so willing to continue in a conflict when he'd already won part of it by not having his son named Collin. Shona didn't understand why he couldn't negotiate on Ryan's middle name.

Shona believes she wouldn't have lingering resentment if she had stuck to her guns on at least one of the name issues. After all, a little conflict wasn't going to kill her or the relationship. For his part, her ex-husband could have been a little more flexible and tried to understand that negotiating over the name of his son didn't mean he was being dominated.

Unfortunately, this is how a lot of couples interact —the woman stews silently after compromising and feeling her partner didn't meet her halfway, and the man refuses to budge on his original decision because he doesn't want to feel he's been defeated.

⋘

You may recognize some or all of these communication patterns in your relationship with your partner. But it's important to remember that that's all they are —conversation patterns. In the end, they don't necessarily signify fundamental differences in values or goals, just different ways of getting there that are equally valid.

One thing we haven't seen any research on is the male addiction to TV remote controls. Our theory is that men are hard-wired to exhibit this particular trait, and women are hard-wired to find it irritating. We are no different. Many times, John flicks through channels endlessly, never deciding on one for more than about three minutes at a time. This habit drives Shona bananas and she frequently gives up and leaves the room in frustration. In his defence, John has modified his behavior by trying hard to avoid flicking through channels until Shona goes to the bathroom or during commercials. This keeps Shona's frustration level low and John feels good because he gets his channel flicking fix.

One male colleague of Shona's laughed out loud as she complained about this at work one day, noting that he had solved that particular conflict in his house by purchasing a large screen TV on which he could display the channel he was watching *plus* two other channels on smaller screens within the large screen! That way, his wife could watch what she wanted on the large screen and he could happily drop in on other channels at the same time.

The reason we bring this up is, although we haven't seen any research on it, we're sure there a scientific basis for men's insistence on continuous surfing. Here's why we think that. One day, John was watching television with then four-year-old Kate. He was engaging in his usual flicking spree, endlessly surfing from channel to channel. After tolerating this for about five minutes, Kate finally said, with a note of desperation in her voice, "Daddy, *please*! Just pick a channel!" John laughed and Shona got great satisfaction out of the fact that she now had company in her frustration.

One last note. Just because these differences are based on extensive studies of male and female communication patterns, they are generalizations. There will always be differences, adaptations, and flexible styles on the part of both genders. Personality styles, which we will discuss later on, are often greater predictors of behavior than gender. Even then, the science of human behavior is fascinating but not necessarily exact. It is interesting and useful, however, to be aware of some common cross-gender communication themes that may challenge you in your blended family. If you're interested in learning more about cross-gender communication, we have noted a number of great references in the *Resources* section of this book. Remember, the success of your blended family starts, first and foremost, with your success as a couple. If you've got some communication challenges between the two of you, work on those diligently as a means of helping the entire family communicate better.

Chapter Ten

Tune Into Your Family's Radio Station

People can only hear you when they are moving toward you, and they are not likely to when your words are pursuing them. Even the choicest words lose their power when they are used to overpower.[1]
　　　　　- Edwin H. Friedman

Weowe a lot of ideas in this chapter and in the whole section on Communication to colleagues and friends Gail Roberts and Bart Mindszenthy, communication specialists.[2] Over the years they have developed some highly effective approaches to organizational communication that we have found work equally well in a blended family situation.

Given that you can't change people, how *do* you begin to influence positive change within your blended family? After all, you are still the parents, and you have a responsibility to raise all of the children with a sense of values, self-responsibility, and respect for others. You also have the right to create your vision for the family and how everyone will live together. The answer is that you start by appealing to something called personal impact.

The WIFM approach

Personal impact is basically about people's self-interest. In other words, no matter who we are, we tend to assess any given situation based on how it's going to affect us. You've probably heard this referred to before as the "What's In It for Me?" (WIFM) perspective. An easy way to remember this — and one we've heard many people use over the years — is that people, including your family members, are constantly tuned into their own private radio station, WIFM. When Mom or Dad says something, I hear it on that frequency. When my partner wants to change something in the blended family, I am tuned into my own channel of WIFM.

Station WIFM may sound a little selfish, but it's really human nature. You may recall learning about Maslow's Hierarchy of Needs when you were in school.[3] Abraham Maslow was an American psychologist who first proposed a model of human needs that describes how people navigate through the world, ensuring we survive and hopefully, thrive. The bottom rung of the human needs ladder is security — having a roof over our heads, getting enough to eat, etc. Once we get those needs met, we begin to move up the ladder with increasingly more socially sophisticated needs. All of them are designed to help us meet whatever needs are important to us as individuals and to help us ensure our own survival.

Once basic survival needs are met, WIFM kicks in on a very individualized basis. Not having phone service is going to have an immediate personal impact on station WIFM for your teenagers, but your eight-year-old probably won't even notice. Cooking spicy Mexican food for your new stepchildren is going to have personal impact for them if they're not used to eating it, but it's also going to have personal impact on you because you're not used to people refusing to eat your cooking. Same situation — different impact. This is station WIFM at work in your blended family.

When considering each new element or issue that arises in your blended family, it's useful to continually analyze each person's WIFM frequency. How is each family member going to react? What aspect of their self-interest will be threatened by the issue? What reactions and emotions can you expect? In other words, put yourself in the shoes of your partner or stepchild and anticipate how you would feel if it happened to you. This simple process goes a long way in helping you deal with inevitable conflicts and concerns in your blended family.

When John and Rudie moved in with Shona and Ryan, Rudie's immediate personal impact was being separated from her friends. Her WIFM station was constantly focusing on this loss. Recognizing this, we ensured that Rudie had her own phone line with a long distance plan installed so she could keep that lifeline open until she adjusted to life in her new town and made new friends.

Similarly, Ryan was concerned that by having to give up his current room to the new baby and Rudie moving into the only extra bedroom, he would have no space for himself. Understanding Ryan's WIFM frequency, John spent the month before Kate was born (during which Ryan was visiting his dad) building a new bedroom for him. The day Ryan arrived home, his room was completely finished, painted, bed made with his favorite blanket and all of his stuff set up. He could pick up exactly where he left off prior to his vacation.

Another WIFM issue for Ryan was his new siblings. Recognizing that it is tough for any child to go from being the only one and having Mom's undivided attention to having three older siblings and a baby sister, we made sure to protect Mom/son rituals important to him. A significant ritual in Ryan's mind was his nightly routine with Mom. Every night since he was very young, Shona would lie on Ryan's bed a few minutes before lights out, and they would read, talk about their days, or just generally chat about things Ryan had on his mind. This was a routine that we did not deviate from, despite the other changes going on in the house. We feel this gave Ryan a sense of security despite all the changes swirling around him. As he grew, of course, this routine gradually died out as it would in any intact family as children mature.

Be sure to attend to the WIFM issues for your partner as well, not just the children. This can include everything from how you're going to feel when your new partner disciplines your children (even if you've agreed you will proceed that way), to how you're going to decorate your now joint bedroom. It's an important conversation and a great time to connect and communicate.

One of the benefits of considering which aspect of WIFM family members are tuned into is your ability to anticipate issues that may or will become a problem. Understanding each person's personal impact won't necessarily change his or her reaction, but you'll be prepared for it and will have had time to create a plan. When your partner and children see, over time, that you've carefully thought through their concerns, you will build a sense of comfort, confidence, and trust. These feelings are important in every family but are particularly important in a blended one. It doesn't mean everything will always go their way; it does mean they will feel respected because you've considered their concerns.

The danger of not tuning into your family's WIFM station is that you will create unnecessary conflict and bad feeling. One thing we see a lot of parents of blended families doing, particularly at the beginning, is trying to convince everyone the blended family will be wonderful and happy. This is the ultimate goal, of course, but no amount of trying to convince your children is going to work until they actually see it for themselves. There is a whole range of WIFM issues that will need to be addressed before your family will ever get to the point of feeling complete comfort, confidence, and trust. After all, this whole blended family thing is *your* idea and decision, not theirs, and the last thing they want to hear once you've made the announcement is how good it's going to be. You have had a lot longer to think about and get used to the idea then they have —they're just hearing about it now. They need at least as long as you've had to process it, if not longer.

A positive and productive approach to tuning into your family's WIFM station is using the Family Meeting we described in Chapter Five. It allows you to lay out your thoughts and reflections as well as listen to theirs. Be sure to start with all the issues and concerns you believe are on the children's minds (their WIFM issues) and also ask if there's something you've missed. Once you've got that straight, the next stage is for you, as the parents and change managers, to explain the plan you have in place to address everyone's concerns. In other words, you provide as much information as possible to help them be clear about and understand how you're going to proceed.

Don't try to convince them

The next step in this process is critical: don't try to convince them. Once you've laid out the plan, give them time to think about it. They will have some questions immediately at the Family Meeting, but many feelings and questions will actually come up after the fact. They need time to make it part of their reality, figure out any other WIFM issues, and come back to you with them. This is all normal. When they come back to you with additional WIFM issues, approach them in exactly the same way as the other issues: listen, ask for time to reflect yourself, and come back with some ideas for a workable plan. If you have older children, figure out the plan together.

It's important to remember that not all issues will be resolved to your children's liking and they may not agree with you. You are not going to please everyone all the time. In fact, you're going to make a whole range of decisions, including forming your blended family in the first place, that your children will neither like nor agree with. Your job is not to convince them to do either. Your job is to be fair and respectful by addressing their WIFM issues as much as possible. Children are no different than any other human being — if they feel they have been listened to, their ideas given due consideration, and a decision made taking those things into account, they can generally accept the outcome, even if it doesn't go their way. The trick is to be consistent about how you deal with their WIFM issues. Sometimes it *will* go their way, and if you're diligent about doing this, they'll have confidence their point of view will be seriously considered and will more easily accept decisions that aren't in their favor.

The powerful thing about addressing WIFM issues and

not trying to convince them your decision is the right one is that you have not robbed them of one of the greatest of personal dignities: the exercise of personal power and the belief they have a choice. It is always a delicate balancing act in parenting in a blended or any other type of family. The ultimate paradox in not trying to convince people to change to your way of seeing things is that they will often (miraculously) decide to change for themselves — simply because you've afforded them the freedom to do so.

Here's an example. When Kate was five she decided she wanted to grow her hair long. Up to that point, we had it styled in a just-below-the-ear cut. But after starting kindergarten, she noticed a lot of girls in her class had much longer hair than her.

Kate has very thick and abundant hair and even with a relatively short haircut it would regularly get tangled and matted. We warned her that long hair would take a lot of care including brushing it morning and night, putting it up in pony tails and braids, etc. We told her it was going to be quite problematic. Naturally she made all kinds of intense promises about future hair care and how diligent she would be. As it was not an important enough issue to expend tons of energy on, we relented and agreed she could grow her hair long.

Of course everything we knew would happen has happened. She forgets to brush her hair on a regular basis, insists on wearing it down instead of in pigtails or a pony tail, and then suffers the painful consequences of Mom brushing out all the tangles at night. Kate does not have a high pain tolerance so she finds these sessions quite torturous.

Neither one of us has ever said 'I told you so', but after several painful hair brushing incidents, including one where Shona had to actually cut a chunk of hair out because it was so badly tangled, we didn't have to. Kate simply announced one night that she wanted to get her hair cut shorter. We said okay and made no comment, but she later said to Shona, "I'm just finding my hair gets tangled too often. I think having it shorter would be easier". Shona simply replied, "Good thinking Kate".

You can also use the concept of WIFM when trying to teach

your children, younger and older, things like self-responsibility and consequences. We recall one period of time when, no matter what we did, Ryan wilfully disregarded rules of behavior at school. We had parent-teacher meetings, we took away his television privileges, banned him from using the computer, limited his playtime with friends —all to no avail. He simply didn't respond to any of our actions. One day, we finally figured out what *really* had personal impact for Ryan: his Game Boy and his Beanie Baby toys. It became clear to us that the thought of losing one of those was quite distressing for him.

We sat him down that night and explained that we knew he knew the rules of the classroom and had proven in the past that he could abide by them. We explained all the reasons why he needed to abide by them for the hundredth time, but this time we made it clear that if he misbehaved again, he was going to lose his Game Boy —not for a day, not for a week, not for a month —forever. He was distraught. But he was also finally prepared to listen. We didn't say anything different than we had the last thirty times we had discussed it with him. The difference was we had his attention.

All of this sounds wonderful, of course, until they test you. And they will. Ryan was great for about three weeks, and then one day it all fell apart. He had a horrible day at school and the teacher was beside herself trying to get Ryan to conform to the classroom rules. After weeks of good behavior, it was obvious Ryan knew exactly what to do —he had just chosen not to do it. Consequently, when he got home, he was quietly told to bring his Game Boy upstairs. Weeping and wailing ensued, but we were resolute. The next day, John and I made arrangements to give the Game Boy away to another boy, and that evening the boy arrived at the front door to collect the Game Boy. Ryan had the job of handing it to him.

Using WIFM for discipline and rewards

When it comes to using WIFM in disciplinary situations, you absolutely have to be willing to follow through. If you don't, your credibility is shot. Was it painful? Totally. Not only for Ryan, but for Shona (remember, she's the big softy). In fact, even writing about this story makes Shona feel bad all over again. That's the great thing about moms: they are wonderful nurturers and they genuinely don't like it when their children feel pain. But of course, being a good parent means you sometimes have to make the tough decisions too. The result of this incident was that Ryan completely trusted that we were serious about such things. From that day on, he knew we weren't bluffing, which was one of the most positive outcomes of that situation.

Even better, Ryan saw the entire situation as one managed jointly by Mom and Step dad —a united front. While it may seem strange, he was also a lot more comfortable with knowing his boundaries. Children, especially strong-willed ones, respond well to structure and clear, predictable rules. This is especially important in building comfort, confidence, and trust in your blended family. We have always been struck by Ryan's good mood when he is in trouble and has a workday imposed upon him. This is a full day of Ryan completing extra chores we assign to him. Frequently, he whistles the entire day and displays an incredibly happy demeanor. We have often been perplexed at his attitude, given the fact the workday is a disciplinary consequence. It reinforces our belief that children are happiest when they've got structure and are clear on the rules.

None of this means that WIFM issues stay the same over time. The Beanie Baby toys no longer hold any big attraction for Ryan so he would feel little personal impact if one were taken away from him today. Now, he responds much more readily to losing time on his favorite computer game. It's not that taking away toys and privileges from children is a new thing, it's just that you have to be willing to follow through with exactly what you said you would do plus you have to be willing to up the stakes (you don't lose your Game Boy for a week, you lose it forever).

Keep in mind that WIFM works just as well in a reward situation as it does in a disciplinary one. For example, Ryan gets computer time *added* to his daily allotment (he's usually allowed one hour maximum) for good behavior, attitude, helpfulness, etc. This gives him something to work toward.

Remember, too, that different children have different WIFM issues. Kate couldn't care less if she lost computer games or Beanie Baby toys. But if you tell her she can't attend her play date with a friend you'd think we ruined her life, and the same with her favorite TV show. Pay attention to what's important to your children. It will get their attention if they feel they might lose it or gain more of it. We often think we know what is important to the children but we can be mistaken. You have to observe carefully and take your cues from the choices they make. It will give you a lot of information about what's *currently* important to them as that constantly shifts with children. What's important to them may well seem silly to you, but in this case, what you care about is irrelevant. In the next chapter we're going to go into more detail on how to take action using WIFM.

Our philosophy on child rearing is that when the children are young, they need a lot more structure, constraints, and formal consequences for their behavior. As they become teenagers, that structure gets gradually relaxed. We have found that this is completely opposite to how many parents deal their teenagers. They can actually become quite restrictive because, of course, the stakes get a great deal higher when your teenagers make mistakes (drinking and driving, becoming pregnant) than what they were when they were ten (staying out past dinnertime, not making their bed five days in a row). The bottom line is, though, that by the time your children are teenagers, you have pretty much taught them the values, rules, and standards of behavior that are healthy and acceptable. As they enter the inevitable stage of directly separating their identity from you, all you really have left is moral authority. If you haven't built moral authority in the years before your child became a teenager, it's not impossible but it is incredibly difficult for you to do it then.

We see understanding the WIFM approach as a way to communicate as your primary tool in building moral authority in your blended family. Naturally, you have to handle it differently depending on the age of your children; four-year-olds respond quite differently than twelve-year-olds. Ultimately, however, tuning into your family's radio station carefully and purposefully will build the comfort, confidence, and trust all of you need to thrive in a blended family.

Chapter Eleven

Stop Talking

Many attempts to communicate are nullified by saying too much.[1]

    - Robert Greeleaf

N ot talking may strike you as a strange way to achieve effective communication in your blended family, but bear with us for a minute. We don't suggest you stop talking altogether as openly discussing issues is a key communication skill in life, let alone in your blended family. Having said that, we know that many people keep talking long after discussion has served its purpose. Discussing reactions and opinions will ensure you remain transparent and allow you to resolve conflict, but when it's time to resolve lingering issues, talking doesn't always get you what you need.

So if talking doesn't work, what does? Action. And action comes from a two-step process: Establishing your *Do Line* and Becoming an *Action Hero*.

Establishing your "Do Line"

At the height of the Cold War in the 1960s, the United States and Canadian governments set up an early warning system across Alaska and the Canadian Arctic called the DEW (Distant Early Warning) Line. Its purpose was to provide quick and decisive communication regarding an impending attack by the Soviet Union. Similarly, we are proposing that you set up your own personal "Do Line" — a boundary that will serve not only as a signal to your blended family that you are finished talking, but as a protection against invasion of your own personal needs and requirements. Simply put, your *Do Line* is the point where you will cease discussion and take action.

To establish your Do Line, you must first identify the events that will trigger its implementation. For the United States and Canada, it was any violation of air space or land that signalled an impending attack. In a nuclear world, they couldn't afford to take any chances that the Soviet Union was bluffing; as a parent, you can't afford to take any chances that your personal boundaries and authority are being eroded. If you do, you are asking for trouble from your children as well as your stepchildren.

In your case, you are not facing immediate nuclear annihilation, but you are facing the distinct possibility that you will never have the moral authority you will need as your children get older and replace you with their friends as the center of their universe. This is particularly true with stepchildren because as you move into the parent/friend role (or already have that role), all you really have is moral authority. They simply *must* see that you are a person who commands respect because you refuse to be manipulated or have your own boundaries violated. This will pay extremely positive dividends with your biological children as well.

Your early warning system may be one thing or a combination of factors: frustration, anger, irritation, despair, yelling, stress, physical symptoms, feeling at your wit's end, constantly feeling hurt, etc. It's going to be unique to each individual, and it's going to take some trial and error for you to observe what sets you off and why, and anticipating events that will potentially cause those feelings. The first step in establishing your Do Line is naming your feelings as they're good indicators of boundary violations. It helps to keep a specific situation in mind. Here's an example.

A few years ago, one of John's sons was attending college. Like many students, he was constantly shifting roommates, requiring numerous moves. This also required our truck. Health issues prevented John from helping, so it fell to Shona to assist in loading and unloading the furniture.

That fall, he had had particularly bad roommate luck, and Shona found herself in the moving industry's version of the movie *Groundhog Day,* meaning she kept moving over and over again. After all of that, coupled with a busy work and family schedule, she had been looking forward to a weekend with nothing scheduled, determined to spend the following one eating chocolates, soaking in a luxurious bath, and reading trashy novels. Wouldn't you know it, though, on Wednesday night, the phone rang. John's son required urgent moving help that weekend.

Here was a Do Line issue for Shona. To manage the situation effectively, she needed to figure out her feelings clearly. In this case, she felt resentful, taken advantage of, and just plain tired. If it's hard accessing your feelings, here's a quick way to identify Do Line issues: If something energizes you and you're excited and happy about it, it's probably not a Do Line issue. If something drains you and it always feels like a struggle, it may well be a Do Line issue. Once you've figured out what drains you, you can move into making a list of all the feelings that arise in that situation.

Becoming an Action Hero

After you've consulted your Do Line and realize you are experiencing strong emotions, start talking. When you've talked for a while and there's no measurable difference in behavior, it's time to take action.

At one point, we had reached the end of our rope regarding lights being turned off. No matter how much we begged the four older children, they wouldn't do it. It's not that they had bad intentions, it's just that the high cost of electricity had no impact on them. Our six-year-old was the only child who was meticulous in turning off lights. Clearly, we weren't tuning into their WIFM frequency.

We found that no one in the family took us seriously until we actually put our money where our mouth was and *did something*. So we instituted a fine system. We announced that anyone who left lights on in rooms they weren't currently using would have to pay five dollars. We figured it was the only way our children would be able to connect their choices with our bills (WIFM).

Things went well for a couple of weeks until someone forgot. We found the lights on in the family room long after everyone had gone to bed, and we knew which two children were responsible. The next morning, we calmly requested five dollars. There was no emotion, no recriminations, just a simple request for payment. They didn't think we were serious. That's the consequence of having talked about something too long —no one believes you mean it. After they realized we did, they paid the fine, and never left the lights on again. Teenagers don't like it when you cut into their fun money.

People respond immediately when you become an Action Hero because they're forced to confront the situation. What action should you take? It all depends on the issue. If you want your partner to help more around the house, burning the bed is a little extreme. Your actions should be logical consequences specifically related to the issue in question. If your teenager constantly brings back the car empty, he needs to buy gas before he's allowed to use it again; if your children consistently refuse your requests to put their dirty clothes in the laundry hamper, you can either stop doing their laundry, require that they do the laundry themselves from now on (a standing rule in our house the minute you turn fourteen), or you can go as far as promising to donate any clothes you find on the floor to the Goodwill.

Of course, sometimes it's not that clear-cut. Take the example of John's son always wanting Shona to help him move. Clearly, the consequence should be that Shona doesn't help him move exactly when *he* wants her to. But taking action based on Do Lines can be difficult. Here's the continuation of that situation.

Firm in her resolve to take a weekend for herself, Shona refused to help him move. She said she would be happy to help the following week, but had plans this weekend.

"What plans?" he demanded.

"Plans to relax," Shona said. "I've been very busy and I need to decompress." She described her sloth fest.

"Those aren't plans," he replied. "That's just sitting around doing nothing. I'm sure you can find time to help me move."

There's always a moment of truth in your Do Line. It's when you hesitate because you feel guilty that you actually had the temerity to tell someone no. You also need to know your Do Line comes with a warning: when you start using it, people get upset. This is because you're inconveniencing them or causing them pain. Go back to Chapter 6 and diagnose your intention. It was not Shona's intention to inconvenience her stepson; she wasn't aware of his moving needs until *after* she had made her plans. Not only that, she had clearly been available to help him on numerous occasions. Objectively, she had nothing to feel guilty about.

John's son was definitely upset. He had a hard time understanding that Shona needed to relax so she could recharge and reengage in all the demands a busy family coupled with a hectic work life can bring. But he got over it and, even better, he found someone else to help him. And you know what? It hasn't harmed their relationship in the least.

When you start becoming and Action Hero based on your Do Lines, most of the time you'll find it only takes once and they'll understand you're serious. Just a reminder from the last chapter: for any of this to work *you can't bluff*. If you said you were going to donate your teenager's hastily-discarded-and-unclean-clothes-after-one-month-on-the-floor to the Goodwill, you *have* to do it. If you don't follow through, nobody will have any reason to take you seriously.

And don't worry about not being nice. You either accept *now* there are times you can't be nice, or you'll find yourself being very not nice during heated conflicts. One thing that often happens when people haven't clearly defined their Do Lines —and no amount of talking has helped —is that anger takes over. They have taken it and taken it, and then one day, they just can't take it any more. Tragically, those are often the points where irreparable damage is caused in family relationships or worse, one of the partners files for divorce. Sometimes you have to do something you don't want to do so you don't have to keep doing it.

Creating a Family Pact

One very effective way to set up clear rules, boundaries, and consequences is to create a *Family Pact*. This is a tool that allows you to head off most issues before they develop or address unanticipated issues as they occur. We have a free Family Pact workbook you can download from our website, www.yoursminehours.com, but read on for the details of putting together this important document.

We've talked about establishing your Do Line and how to become an Action Hero to effect change in your blended family, but it wouldn't be fair to suddenly spring those actions on people without any warning. That's where creating a Family Pact comes in, a clearly defined set of expectations and obligations of and to each other that everyone agrees to live by, as well as consequences when you don't live up to the agreement. If someone doesn't live up to it, that's when your Do Line and Action Hero tactics become operational.

Why is a Family Pact necessary? Why can't you just all get along? Well, it's simple. Even if you all get along really well at the beginning, after a few months of living together the idiosyncrasies of the other family begin to come out. It's not that you didn't notice them before, it's just that now what seemed tolerable or even cute begins to irritate you. Remember the story of Rudie taking Shona's wet laundry out of the washing machine and dumping it on the dryer so she could do her own clothes? It started out as something Shona was willing to tolerate, but very soon it became a major annoyance. Now multiply something like that small issue by several more people, add a dash of different family culture, and a whole range of other habits from eating to neatness to bedtime hours and it gets really crazy, really fast.

One of the reasons a Family Pact is a particularly powerful tool in a blended family is because you are dealing with people whose personalities are not second nature to you. While a Family Pact can be just as useful in an intact family, it is an immediately powerful mechanism in a blended family in that it helps you handle all the unanticipated conflicts and misunderstandings that you don't necessarily have in an intact family because you have all grown up together.

Having romantic notions that your blended family is going to be *so happy* is setting yourself up for a crisis of expectation, which is where a lot of our reactions originate when we get into conflict with others. Our observation is that most conflict arises out of one person having one set of expectations, the other person having no clue about those expectations —or having a totally different set of expectations —and then their worlds collide because they weren't clear with each other.

Our Family Pact actually started with a set of ground rules we developed for ourselves as a couple. It taught us that clear expectations and consequences, and a clear understanding of those expectations and consequences was critical to the health of our relationship. Here's what we mean.

When we decided to move in together, we sat down to articulate ground rules for living with each other. John explained that, during his marriage to his first wife, he had asked her and the three children to never take coins from a plastic bank in which he deposited his spare change.

"I know it seems a little trivial," John said at the time, "but it's a rather large bank, and I have this silly little goal of seeing how much I can actually save when the bank is full. I made this clear to my ex-wife and the children, but they never respected it and were forever raiding my bank for spare change for whatever —the bus, an ice cream, a CD —whatever they felt they just *had to have* at the time but couldn't afford. I know it's just a change bank, but it's also a symbol of respect for my personal wishes, and I always felt like that was constantly violated by them."

The consequence for John was that he lost faith and trust in his family on that particular issue. The consequence for the rest of the family was John became very guarded about his spare change.

John then asked Shona if she could respect his wishes not to have change borrowed from his bank, and she agreed. Two years later, when we finally decided to get married on a trip in Greece, John dumped out his now full bank, counted it up, and the total came to just over $500.

"What are you going to do with that money?" Shona asked, fully expecting that John would treat himself to something he wanted.

"I'm going to take it to Greece," he said. While Shona insisted that he should use it for something special just for him, John insisted that he wanted nothing more than to use it to do fun things on the trip. So, with an extra $500 in our pocket, we had an extra great time in Greece! The moral of the story? Respect for other people's wishes reaps great benefits for you as well. In other words, the consequence in this case was a very positive one!

After John had made his bank wishes clear, it was Shona's turn. "Any boundaries you don't want me to violate?" asked John.

"Well, it's not so much a boundary as it is just a reality about me you will have to accept," Shona replied. John looked quizzical, wondering what it could possibly be. "Here's the bold-faced truth," she began, "I cannot be trusted alone in the house with chocolate." John laughed. Shona looked serious.

"During the time I've known you, I have noticed you are in the habit of purchasing chocolate bars and leaving them lying around for weeks in your car or your house. Sometimes you even leave them for months!" Shona exclaimed.

"I like to have them handy in case I get a sweet craving," John explained.

"I know that", said Shona, "but here's the thing...There is no way that any of your chocolate bars will survive longer than about a day in a house with me. I cannot control myself when it comes to chocolate. Consequently, the ground rule I need you to live by is this: if you buy a chocolate bar and I find it I will eat it. Not in a week. Not in a month, but in the moment I find it. And I'm not fussy. It doesn't much matter which chocolate bar it is, and it doesn't much matter if it's in the living room, your car, your bedside table, whatever. If I see it, I will eat it. Also, if you have purchased chocolate for baking such as chocolate chips or baker's blocks —and in the absence of any chocolate bars in the house —I will eat those too. I need you to accept this fact and never have an expectation there will chocolate in the house longer than a twenty-four-hour period, if that. Can you live with that?"

"Yes, I can live with that," replied John, a small smile on his face.

"I'm serious," Shona reiterated. "This means that, now that you have agreed to this and understand it, when I do eat your chocolate bars in the future, you cannot get mad. You cannot hold it against me. You cannot in any way show irritation at the situation." We both agreed and went on to discuss other minor issues such as John's knuckle cracking and Shona's nail biting, all of which has worked nicely for us ever since.

This description of our conversation is the same process you will work through in creating a Family Pact. First, you state your expectations of the other person. Once he or she agrees to live by this expectation, it becomes an obligation to do so simply because the person has willingly and consciously accepted the terms. Not only that, you'll notice that the exact *meaning* of the expectations were spelled out.

In John's case, he didn't just ask Shona to refrain from taking coins from his bank. He explained the background of why it was so important to him and all the circumstances he could think of under which taking money would be unacceptable. "Under any circumstances" may have done the trick, but people being people, we can often rationalize that the other person didn't actually *mean* such an extreme statement when we want to violate it.

In Shona's case, she was very clear that not only would she eat chocolate John left lying around, she would eat any kind of chocolate, any time, any place. She also emphasized that, having agreed that he could live with that, John could not now get upset or blame Shona for it in any way. The expectations were clear, but so were the obligations.

In creating a pact that governs your whole family, everyone gets a chance to state their expectations of how the family will live together. They explain why those expectations are important to them and what it looks like when people live by them.

For example, we stated that no one was allowed to enter another person's room without knocking first. This applied to everyone, regardless of age. We had had some issues with Ryan barging into Rudie's room while she was changing. However, we had also had some issues where the older children had done the same thing to Ryan, thinking it couldn't possibly matter to a six-year-old. We explained that respect is respect, no matter what the age of the child. It was important to Ryan and the cohesiveness of our family that he be afforded the same basic rights and responsibilities as the older children. Notice we said *basic*. Obviously there are a number of rights and responsibilities that are clearly age-appropriate. In any case, we made our thinking transparent regarding why knocking on doors was an important standard in our Family Pact. We also explored consequences for not sticking to this rule, such as the offended child got to walk into your room unannounced for the next day, or the same child got to play with a treasured game or toy belonging to you.

The Wiggle Room

Why is it so important for you to provide the background and thinking behind each element plus define consequences in your Family Pact? Because you have to make sure people aren't living in what we call the *Wiggle Room*. The Wiggle Room isn't an actual physical space in your house, but a psychological space in your children's minds that allows them to talk their way out of experiencing consequences for their own choices. Here's what we mean.

If we say it's important to knock on people's doors because it's respectful, but we don't add that it applies to people of all ages, then the older children have Wiggle Room to be able to escape consequences. "I didn't realize the rule applied to *everyone*," they can argue, explaining that they believed young children didn't need privacy. And you know what? They'd be right. You didn't explain clearly that your view was children of all ages deserved such respect, so you now have no right to administer consequences for violation of the rule. Of course, some rules are more clear-cut than others — you may not take other children's toys without permission, for example — but there is a lot of room for debate on issues that aren't that clear.

Many parents unwittingly build a Wiggle Room for their children by not being crystal clear about expectations, obligations, and consequences. They then find themselves in endless negotiations, arguments, and he said-she said situations with their children that are hard to resolve because no one will take responsibility for the issue, including the parents. The Family Pact is the perfect accountability tool for children and parents alike, a sort of wrecking ball for the Wiggle Room where all the children's objections and attempted manipulations of the situation come crashing down around them and they are left exposed to the light of day.

Another example of something we put in our Family Pact was the issue of picking up after each other. At first, we had simply asked people to put their stuff away. Sometimes they did, sometimes they didn't. When they did, it was to the letter of the law — they'd put their own stuff away but continue to trip over someone else's stuff and take no action whatsoever. At some point, asking turned into begging and pleading for the children to put their school things away as soon as they got home. Despite frequent requests, however, we were constantly tripping over backpacks, discarded lunch bags, text books, you name it. We addressed this in preparing our Family Pact by not only saying everyone had to pick up after themselves, we made it crystal clear what that looked like: "If you walk, trip, or otherwise run into an item in any common space in the house *more than twice*, put it away. *It doesn't matter if this item belongs to you or not.* Just put it away. If you don't know who it belongs to, find out. If he or she is not home, put it in his or her room." We allowed people to trip over things twice before taking action to give the real offender a chance to put his or her own stuff away.

There are two sets of consequences for not picking up after yourself. First, in the event someone else has to put away your stuff — and that someone else is a sibling — they may well just dump your things unceremoniously on your bedroom floor. This often resulted in belongings getting damaged. After several incidents of this, those who valued their belongings ensured they put them away properly. Second, if you don't care about your belongings getting damaged and continue to count on other people to put your things away, you lose privileges, such as computer time, television shows, etc., or whatever appeals to the WIFM of that particular child.

❧

Basically, a Family Pact involves documenting and defining a clear set of expectations and obligations everyone has of and to each other plus any consequences for non-compliance. If you like, it's simply a set of ground rules that all of you agree you can live with, with the distinction being that not only do you list the standards of behavior, you clearly define what that behavior looks like. A *shared and common* understanding of the ground rules and consequences is absolutely essential. If you stop at having created the list without hashing out with everyone what each item on the list actually looks like in practice, what you have is a beautiful set of Motherhood and Apple Pie statements that sound nice but don't really have any teeth.

Oh...by the way. Shona remained true to her word and does eat all of the chocolate bars John brings into the house. He did try some adaptive behaviors, such as hiding the chocolate behind books and under papers, but invariably, Shona would find them and would eat them. True to his word, John never has become irritated, but they did amend the Pact somewhat to note that when Shona does find John's hidden chocolate, she has a responsibility to inform him that the chocolate was found and duly devoured. That way he knows he needs to replenish his supply. A Family Pact should always be a living document that can be renegotiated depending on how the original terms are being lived out and what new things may need to be added.

That's another element of the Family Pact: you never have to say I told you so. You also don't have to get into yelling matches and power struggles and protracted debates. Instead, everything is calmly and rationally set out, and your children have nothing to push against because they have previously agreed to the elements of the Pact. This doesn't mean to suggest that you will not encounter situations not covered by the Pact. You will, and the last thing you want to do is start developing long lists of do's and don'ts (highly inappropriate anyway seeing as every child is unique). What it will have done is develop your skills, and those of your children and stepchildren, to be able to calmly identify mutual expectations and obligations and what you all know the consequences will be.

Building self-responsibility

One element of our Family Pact was a formal list of housework rules and consequences for non-compliance posted on the fridge. One child in the family was quite offended by this. He told us we were going over the top and why couldn't we just talk about it? When we responded that four months of talking about it hadn't changed his behavior, we made our point. He hadn't been taking responsibility for one of his roles in the family.

One of the universal issues we face in raising children involves teaching them a sense of personal responsibility. Our job is to help them understand that for every choice they make and action they take, there is a set of reactions that will occur in response. One of the greatest teaching strengths of the Family Pact is that there is absolutely no doubt for your children that they have choices, but there is also absolutely no doubt that there are consequences resulting from their choices (some good, some bad, some neutral). The Family Pact is one of your best tools for teaching your children and stepchildren a sense of self-responsibility.

Let's examine a rule we have in our house regarding body piercings. When Rudie was seventeen, she badgered us for months to allow her to get her nose pierced. Her father finally relented one day and allowed it, feeling that it was relatively harmless and recognizing it was a current social trend in young people. (He wasn't *always* a curmudgeon with the teenagers — just about certain things like designer clothes.) Of course, he had already discussed the issue with Shona and had her agreement.

As is typical with all children —and teenagers are masters at it —as soon as she got her nose pierced, the badgering for more stepped up a notch. This time, she wanted permission to get her belly button pierced, and this time, she had a much bigger battle on her hands. At least once a week she would engage us in a debate over why she wasn't allowed, and at least once a week we would reiterate our health concerns over belly button piercing. In the end, John simply stated that while he realized he had an emotionally-based reaction to the thought of his daughter having her belly button pierced —he thought it was gauche, cheap looking, and sent a certain message about her personality that was inconsistent with her true nature —as well as health concerns, the answer was no. Rudie walked away mumbling that when she was eighteen, she was going to go ahead and do whatever she wanted. John agreed that yes, in fact, she would have a right to make her own decisions at eighteen.

A couple of weeks later, the entire family was sitting at the dinner table eating when Rudie, who was wearing a midriff-style shirt, yawned and stretched. That just happened to be the moment when Shona's line of sight hit her belly button —and there was a brand new piercing in all its glory. The table grew quiet as she realized we had discovered her deliberate disregard for our wishes.

Shona calmly asked, "When did that happen?"

Rudie sheepishly replied, "A couple of days ago." John's face looked like thunder. Rudie had clearly violated one of the elements of our Family Pact.

So what can you do when your seventeen-year-old daughter, a few weeks away from her eighteenth birthday, has flaunted your clearly expressed wishes? We go back to Chapter Eight and the Ninth Law of Acceptance —Pick the right hills to die on. Knowing it was a battle already lost, we chose to say nothing, but it was clear that neither one of us was thrilled about the piercing.

A few days later, Shona noticed that Rudie no longer had a belly button piercing. When she asked why, she had the good grace (also part of her nature) to admit that it kept getting infected and besides, it was very uncomfortable to wear under clothes. Many times, the best thing you can do for your children is allow them to experience the consequences of their own choices. Saying "I told you so" is never necessary —you can see it written all over their faces.

But the battle wasn't over yet. The next issue to arise was that of tongue piercing. We guess Rudie figured that seeing as the belly button thing hadn't worked out, she'd go ahead and get barbells in her tongue. Shona was appalled but said nothing, knowing that this would undoubtedly be a hill that John would choose to die on, and he didn't disappoint her.

The main difference between the belly button piercing debate and the tongue piercing debate was a legal one: Rudie had already turned eighteen when she announced she would be getting her tongue pierced, but she was still living at home. John chose to handle it adult-to-adult rather than father-to-daughter, a very smart move with a newly-minted adult.

There was no doubt in Rudie's mind what our opinion would be, and she had clearly chosen it as her first adult battle with Dad and Step mom. To her credit, she made her announcement in a matter-of-fact, mature manner. Her father returned the favor, making it very clear that not only did he not want to witness one of his children deliberately mutilating herself, he especially didn't want to be reminded of it every day, particularly in light of the fact that he had two younger children to worry about. He explained that both of us fundamentally didn't feel it was setting a good example for the kind of lifestyle and values we wanted to teach Ryan and Kate. He quietly and politely set an adult boundary with his newly adult child, and that boundary was it wasn't going to be tolerated in our house.

Unfortunately, Rudie was not prepared for this boundary. "But you said that when I was eighteen I would have the right to do what I want because I would be an adult! Well, now I'm an adult and this is what I want," she said with finality in her voice.

"That's absolutely correct," John replied, "you *are* an adult, but so am I. And as an adult, I am merely being clear about the behavior and values I expect in my own home."

She was quiet for a minute. "So what you're saying is that I *can't* really do what I want even though I'm an adult. You're still acting like my dad!"

John disagreed, "No, I will always defend your right to make your own choices as an adult, and if this is your choice, I won't try to stop you. What I'm saying is that, while adults have the right to make whatever choices they want, *there are always consequences for those choices*. In this case, one of the consequences is that I choose not to have anyone living in my home with such a piercing for reasons I have already explained."

When you think about it, the Family Pact, the concept of tuning into your family's radio station (WIFM), picking the hills to die on, and a whole range of other perspectives we've mentioned all serve to teach your children something about self-responsibility. But it also teaches them that other people have the right to their own expectations, emotional reactions, and issues about which they might not agree with you. When they become adults, leave home, and make a life for themselves, they will encounter very real consequences for their own behavior and choices —ones that you can no longer explain or even protect them from. Your kids don't have to like the consequences of their own behavior but at least you can teach them that they have a choice whether or not they can live with the consequences.

Rudie didn't like the potential consequences of getting her tongue pierced — that her dad and step mom would make the choice not to have their younger children exposed to it and therefore would request that she move out. In the end, she chose not to get her tongue pierced and remained living at home until she moved to Mexico to learn Spanish. That was several years ago, and she has chosen not to have her tongue pierced yet, but she's made that choice as a thinking, self-responsible adult, not as a result of pressure from parents *or* peers.

Part of the problem with trying to build self-responsibility in your children is that you don't necessarily get a lot of support from society these days. Here's an example. When Ryan was about ten, he was going through a phase of extreme forgetfulness. He would neglect to bring home homework assignments, or do them at home but forget to take them to school. He forgot hats, mittens, books, toys; you name it, he was constantly forgetting stuff. We were becoming exasperated with him. No amount of reminding him and helping him develop systems to remember were working. He has no learning disabilities and has absolutely no trouble remembering in intricate detail things he is interested in. He just wasn't choosing to remember these other things. We knew the time had come for Ryan to experience consequences.

One day during this phase, Ryan forgot his lunch. Crying and hungry, he phoned Shona on her cell phone to ask her to bring his lunch to school. She happened to be in the neighboring city attending client meetings and told him no. Even if she had been at home, she would have said no, for we believed the only way that Ryan would take responsibility for himself and his things was to allow him to suffer the consequences of his choices. This situation seemed like a relatively harmless opportunity for him to do so as it clearly wasn't going to kill Ryan to miss one meal.

When Shona got home to greet Ryan after school, she asked him if he wanted a snack. He smugly replied that he wasn't hungry because school staff had heated up a frozen lasagne for him at lunch. It seems the school kept those meals on hand just in case kids forgot their lunches.

We were infuriated! Not only was Ryan robbed of the opportunity to experience the consequences of his own choices, he had now learned he would be bailed out if he did it again. Worse, it was plainly obvious that he knew it.

Shona phoned the principal the next day and explained that school staff was *not* to bail Ryan out again. The response was lukewarm and the principal indicated that staff felt sorry for kids who forgot their lunch and were just trying to be kind. It's important for you to know that we live in a fairly affluent community — not even *one* child is close to being underfed.

We can think of numerous other examples of society not holding our children responsible for their choices: teachers consistently excusing late assignments at school; friends' parents allowing our children to play with toys confiscated due to bad behavior; teenagers' parents buying them a brand new car every few months because they keep crashing the old ones. The point is, we find ourselves in a constant struggle between teaching our children self-responsibility and having them witness a whole range of examples all around them of peers feeling no consequences whatsoever.

Objectively, all of us know that the world does not work that way, that there are all kinds of consequences for our choices and behavior, some minor, some very serious. The sooner your children understand how to deal with them (in age-appropriate ways, of course), the sooner they will be equipped to ably and confidently handle whatever life throws at them. Remember, you children's job is to grow up and leave you. Who are you turning loose on society? A thinking, feeling, contributing individual who takes responsibility for his or her own choices and for making the home/town/country/planet a better place? Or someone who expects a world that owes him or her a living and will come to the rescue whenever things go badly? If it's the latter, he or she is going to be sorely disappointed and experience a great deal of pain.

This is clearly a parenting issue not confined to blended families. Again, however, we believe blended families —because of their complexities and frequent opportunities for continuing conflict —are an ideal place to teach children self-responsibility. Given all of the challenges of a blended family, we can't imagine how we'd survive if people weren't working toward taking responsibility for themselves, children and parents alike. It would be chaos.

Chapter Twelve

Send in the Coach

If you deliberately plan on being less than you are capable of being, then I warn you that you'll be unhappy for the rest of your life.[1]
- Abraham Maslow

Another wonderful tool that will support and enhance your Family Pact as well as further support your stepchildren's and children's growing aptitude for self-responsibility is something called coaching.

Most books we have read about parenting, business communications, management, leadership, relationships, etc. have one thing in common: the belief that building capacity in others to make their own decisions, think for themselves, and gain confidence in their own abilities (relationship or otherwise) is by far the best way to achieve success and a sense of self-efficacy. When you think about, aren't these your goals for your blended family?

To achieve this, what has worked wonderfully well for us is something called the coach approach. Corporate Coach U was, we think, the first to coin this phrase, and it applies very well in a blended family situation.[2] After Shona became a certified coach facilitator through Corporate Coach U, she began facilitating coaching skills in her organization. The more she facilitated the course and the more she was able to practice her own coaching skills, the more she began to see the benefits of adopting the coach approach with the children. (If you're interested in learning more about coaching, either Corporate Coach U or Coach U are wonderful organizations that can help you master the art of coaching your children. See the *Resources* section for more information).

Socrates was right

Basically, using the coach approach means you adopt a questioning rather than a telling approach. If you like, you could refer to it as the Socratic method (Socrates was famous for his teaching style of asking questions rather than simply providing information). What that looks like in the case of parenting is something like this.

Your teenage daughter comes home upset about something that happened at school. Instead of giving her advice on ways she could solve the problem, ask questions instead. Asking her questions that lead her to come up with the solution herself will build far more self-confidence than you trying to solve the problem for her.

Let's take a look at another coaching example. One day shortly after learning her new coaching skills, Shona had the opportunity to put what she had learned to good use. She was on the way to a children's indoor playground with then eight-year-old Ryan and then two-year-old Kate. Ryan had been looking forward to this trip for a week, so he was excited to get in the car. No sooner had they pulled out of the driveway than his analytical little mind went to work.

"Mom, are you sure you know where you're going? Perhaps we should stop at a gas station and get a map." Notwithstanding the fact that we had been to the playground on previous occasions, he was concerned that we might get lost. Mildly irritated, Shona assured him that she knew where she was going. That bought her about twenty seconds of peace. Then the next assault came.

"Mom, are you sure you have enough gas? Perhaps we should fill up the tank before we leave?" Now her teeth were clenched. Being a very different personality style than Ryan — one that usually feels she has the situation in hand — she doesn't react well when it seems like someone is telling her how to do something she knows perfectly well how to do. It especially irks her when it's someone thirty years younger who knows nothing about gas or driving! Taking a deep breath, she calmly assured him that there was enough gas to get them where they wanted to go.

Such conversations and reactions are common between Shona and Ryan. He often strikes Shona as a worry wart — always worrying about details and if everything is organized properly. Many times she has told him that he doesn't have to worry about details like that as being his mom (and a capable adult) she has everything under control. This comment had never worked before, however, and it certainly didn't work on this occasion either (remember the definition of insanity?).

After five minutes of relative silence, Ryan's worrying adopted a new focus: "Mom, what if Kate gets hungry or thirsty while we're at the playground? Are you sure you brought enough bottles for her?" Shona bit back a frustrated response, all of a sudden remembering what she had just learned about coaching. She decided to adopt a coach approach, and instead of arguing with him or getting frustrated, she began asking questions.

"Well, Ryan," she replied, "let's say that I do run out of bottles for the baby. And let's say she does get hungry. How do you think we could handle that situation?"

He went into immediate analysis mode. After musing to himself for a few moments, he replied, "Well, they do have a snack bar at the playground...And they have apple and other juices there, and Kate can drink quite well from a straw now, so I guess we could buy her some apple juice!" Eureka! Problem solved. And best of all, he got there on his own without Shona getting frustrated and ending up telling him to be quiet. But she knew she wasn't out of the woods yet. She asked another question.

"So that covers the thirst issue," she continued. "How about if she gets hungry?"

He took another few seconds to mull this over carefully. "Hmm," Ryan replied. "They *do* sell hotdogs there and Kate *does* like to eat cut-up hotdogs, so we could buy her a hot dog!"

"Exactly!" Shona replied enthusiastically. Through using a coach approach, she had given Ryan space to learn some skills of reasoning for himself. In the process, she saved herself a lot of frustration and irritation.

For the next five minutes they had a relatively peaceful ride, until Ryan's panicked voice screamed from the back seat as if something horrible had suddenly occurred to him.

"Mom!" he cried frantically.

"What?" Shona asked urgently, now concerned Ryan or Kate's life was in imminent danger.

"What if you don't have enough money to pay for the apple juice and hotdog?"

It's a good thing Shona was driving or she's not sure she could have restrained herself from strangling her firstborn on the spot.

Adopting a coach approach in your blended family by asking questions rather than telling usually accomplishes three goals:

1. The person being coached can arrive at an answer, thereby building skills in analysis and a sense of confidence that he or she can handle problems.

2. The other person can diffuse any frustration and potential anger in interacting with the person being coached by focusing on helpful questions rather than reactions.

3. It helps diffuse conflict by focusing on the solution rather than the problem.

In the case of Shona and Ryan's interaction in the car, the coach approach helped Ryan arrive at answers for himself, diffuse Shona's frustration with his communication style, and allowed for a conversation rather than a conflict, with Shona telling Ryan to be quiet and Ryan being offended. It's true that Shona did end up frustrated in the end, but she's learned more since then on how to approach Ryan based on his communication style. We'll talk more about individual styles later in the chapter. For now, let's concentrate on some key coaching skills.

1. Ask thought-provoking questions

When interacting with the members of your blended family (including your partner), where appropriate, ask questions instead of providing advice, telling them what to do, etc. Again, it allows them to think things through and arrive at solutions for themselves. This is a much more powerful way of embedding learning that will be remembered than if you were to just teach or tell.

One question-asking skill Shona learned in her coaching training was to try to avoid the word "why" as much as possible in the body of a question. For example, if your teenage daughter is upset about a fight she had with her girlfriend because she cancelled a Friday-night arrangement with her to go on a date with a boy, and you ask, "Why did you say that to her?" it can often provoke a defensive response. The word why signals to people that they have to defend themselves and provide an explanation. Being in a defensive frame of mind is rarely useful in solving conflict and focusing on solutions. You would probably be more successful if you asked your daughter, "What were the things going through your mind when you spoke with your girlfriend?" That way, you are asking her to provide information —and thus making her thinking transparent—instead of asking her to explain her actions.

A second question-asking skill Shona learned was to not provide the answer to the question in the question itself. Anyone who is a fan of legal shows on TV will know that a common phrase lawyers use in court is "Objection —leading the witness." In the same situation with your teenage daughter, if you ask her, "Do you think canceling your date on Friday so you can go the movies with your girlfriend would help?" you have just put a solution in her head that isn't hers —it's yours. It may well be that you're right and she does need to cancel her date because she made plans with her girlfriend first. But so what? Your daughter hasn't worked out the solution for herself. She hasn't had the opportunity to take self-responsibility for her actions nor have you helped her build capacity for analyzing her behavior and arriving at a solution she is happy with.

2. Become comfortable with silence

When you do ask a coaching question, be prepared to let that person sit with it, thus allowing time to think and process. If you start talking immediately after asking the question, you're not giving the person's brain time to analyze and really answer the question. The answer may well be obvious to you, but it isn't to your child or partner. Give them time to figure it out. Asking them more questions or adding commentary will only distract them.

When teachers are being trained in college they will often learn about the concept of wait time when questioning students. If you force yourself to wait for thirty seconds after asking a question you accomplish two key things: 1. You allow enough time for the other person to process the question and respond thoughtfully, and 2. Because dead air time is uncomfortable, your patience will often encourage the person to answer and fill the silence even when he or she might prefer to remain silent.

3. Talk less, listen more

Another thing Shona learned from Corporate Coach U was something called the 80-20 rule. If your primary role as a coach is to facilitate the other person's capacity for analysis and problem solving, then it makes sense that you should be talking less and listening more during the course of the coaching interaction. This means that the person in whom you are trying to build capacity should be talking more (at least eighty percent of the time) and you as facilitator of that process should be talking less (no more than twenty percent of the time). It's incredibly easy to get drawn into debates and negotiations, especially with children, so if you ask questions, let them sit there in silence while your child or partner considers them, and pay attention to how much talking you are doing in the interaction. You'll be able to gauge how much you're coaching and how much you're actually giving advice. You can bet that if you're doing a lot —or even half —of the talking, you're more in telling mode than coaching mode.

None of this means, however, that there aren't times where it's appropriate to give advice, tell stories, etc. All we're saying is that coaching can provide wonderful opportunities, especially in emotionally-charged and conflict-laden situations, to get people objectively evaluating themselves as well as the situation. They are intelligent enough to figure out the answer; the coach's role is to help them get there. Additionally, we believe as your children get older, you must assume more of a coaching role than a direct parenting role. Remember, once your children are older teenagers, most of your influence comes from the moral authority you have built in the preceding years. Coaching is a wonderful way to remain involved and helpful in their lives while allowing them the freedom as soon-to-be-adults to solve their own problems.

4. Remember your family's radio station

One of the toughest challenges for you when using the coach approach is keeping your own opinions and judgments out of the conversation. Coaching is not about you, your goals, what you wish the kids would do, how you wish things would go. Coaching is all about the person being coached. It requires you to turn off your interests in the conversation —your needs, wants, values, beliefs, personal background, etc. In other words, it requires you to develop detached interest in the conversation and remove your reactions from it. Coaching is actually a powerful way to build a sense of Acceptance of the situation in yourself as well.

Go back to radio station WIFM. Get out of your own mental way and figure out what's important to the person you're coaching and focus on that. Your opinion of his or her emotions, reactions, behaviors, and decisions is irrelevant at this moment. It's his or hers that counts. We know it's difficult to do this, especially with children when you're concerned about situations they have gotten themselves into, but it's often the most productive approach with the least possibility for creating more conflict. Here's an example.

When Rudie decided to move into an apartment in the nearest city, she borrowed a truck from her friend's dad. It was a big, beautiful, brand new truck that would hold most of her furniture in one load. She knew that the truck was this man's baby and he was very careful with it; she also knew he was quite nervous about lending it to an eighteen-year-old. However, he decided to take a chance, believing Rudie would treat it responsibly. They agreed she would pick up the truck on a Saturday morning and she would return it by Sunday afternoon. Rudie spent the weekend moving and both of us watched her take very good care of the truck. We had no doubts she would return it in good shape.

Sunday morning arrived and the entire family happened to be home that weekend, including John's parents visiting from out of town. We took the opportunity to make a nice breakfast and visit with everyone. During the meal, Rudie presented her problem.

It seems that, somewhere along the way, she had sheared the passenger-side side mirror right off the truck. She didn't know where it had happened, other than to offer the observation that the street she was moving to was fairly narrow, with cars and trees on either side. The only thing she could think of was that, somehow, when maneuvering the large truck along this street, she had bashed a tree with the mirror. Taking responsibility for the situation, Rudie explained that she had made an appointment with a garage for later that morning to replace the missing mirror. The garage assured her that the truck would be as good as new, and the owner wouldn't even know there had been a problem. The problem she presented to the family was this: should she tell her friend's dad about the mirror even though it was fixed? Or should she just return the truck and not say a word about it?

A full-fledged family debate followed, with half of us saying she should confess the full story and the other half saying she shouldn't say a word — she had fixed the damage and why cause unnecessary bad feeling? John and Shona were on opposite sides of the issue.

In the end, it was Tim who asked his sister a coaching question that silenced all of us. He asked Rudie what her motivation for not telling would be. Was it to protect the truck owner's feelings or was it to protect herself from an unpleasant reaction? You could have heard a pin drop. In the final analysis, this was an ethical dilemma with no right answer. It didn't matter what any of us thought — and we'd been pretty vocal with our opinions. It only mattered what Rudie thought. The answer to that coaching question would guide her to a course of action she was comfortable with.

In the end, she decided to return the truck without mentioning the mirror. Some of us agreed with that decision, some of us didn't. Neither John nor Shona felt it was a hill to die on, especially with an eighteen-year-old. What's more important are the four things that came out of that situation:

1. Rudie took responsibility for fixing a situation she had caused. We were proud of that, even if some of us didn't agree with all of her decisions.

2. She was comfortable and trusted her entire blended family enough to engage all of us in an ethical debate concerning her. It's moments like that that tell you you've made real progress in establishing a trusting, comfortable environment.

3. It was a great opportunity, especially for the younger

children, to reflect on different values and how there are often no black and white answers. Life is frequently a messy affair.

4. Someone in the family effectively used a coaching approach to diffuse what was becoming a heated situation.

Coaching isn't always going to solve problems and diffuse conflict, but we think it's a powerful place to start, especially with a blended family. Who knows? You might not have to go beyond a coaching conversation because the issue gets resolved.

They're not trying to tick you off on purpose

Remember Shona's interaction with Ryan when she was driving he and Kate to the indoor playground? She used a coach approach to get Ryan to sort out answers for himself while at the same time trying to keep her own frustration with his worry-wart questions down to a manageable level.

A coach approach is indeed a wonderful tool when others' communication styles based on their personalities are very different from your own. They're really not trying to tick you off on purpose, they are just being themselves. No one approach to any given situation is right or wrong — it's just different.

We are definitely a mix of vastly different personalities in our blended family. Some of us are more analytical and detail oriented, others are more outgoing and spontaneous. Whatever the case, it makes for some fairly frustrating interactions when we approach situations using the style that's most comfortable for us. After all, we see the world through a perspective unique to us. The challenge comes when you have to communicate with each other and you're not appreciating that each person needs to receive information in a different way based on personality.

There are a number of personality assessment tools out there that are very useful to a blended family. We've read about most of them as well as taken many different self-assessments to try to better understand each other. Quite honestly, we don't think it matters much which one you choose, but we think it does matter that you choose some kind of assessment. It gives you such a useful language with which you can understand and interpret each other's behavior.

The tool we find easiest to use and understand is called the DiSC® profile, developed by Inscape Publishing and available through our website (www.yoursminehours.com — see *Resources* section).[3] Basically, it identifies four different categories of personality you can expect to encounter in the world and in your blended family — those characterized by Dominance (D), Influence (i), Steadiness (S) and Conscientiousness (C). Often, you are a good mix of two of those categories, but you may well be a mix of all four. Knowing which category best describes each person in your blended family and how they need to be communicated with is extremely helpful in building relationships, resolving conflict, and just plain understanding where someone is coming from.

On the next page, you'll see a diagram of the basic DiSC model. People's personalities tend to diverge along two lines: They're either more active or more thoughtful, and at the same time, they're either more questioning or more accepting. Looking at the DiSC model, you'll see the descriptions of each of those four elements and where each of the four major personality styles (the D, the i, the S, and the C) fit. If you're a D, for example, you will possess elements of both the active and the questioning personalities. If you're an S, you'll possess elements of both the thoughtful and accepting personalities.

If you and your family members fill out a DiSC personality profile, you'll answer a number of questions about how you feel and what you would do in certain situations. You then receive a score that tells you where you sit on each element of the DiSC model. The higher your score in one area, the more that personality style will be evident in your behavior.

In our blended family, we have two strong D's, two strong C's, and three strong i's. However, each one of those personalities comes with a very close second score. Let's take Shona for example. Her highest score is i, so she is a blend of active and accepting qualities. However, her second strongest score is a

D, and it's a very close second. The strong D emphasizes her active qualities plus it adds some questioning qualities as well. Her lowest score is C, which means Shona has very few qualities in the thoughtful category —methodical, careful, and calm are not words anyone would use to describe her! This doesn't mean she can't be all of those things when the situation demands it —she can. It's just not where she naturally goes, or even where she chooses to go.

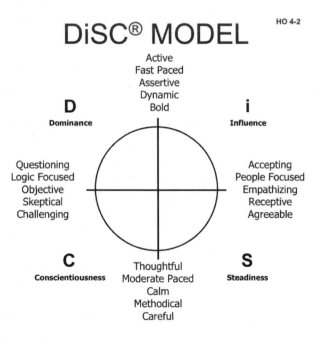

DiSC® MODEL

HO 4-2

Active
Fast Paced
Assertive
Dynamic
Bold

D
Dominance

i
Influence

Questioning
Logic Focused
Objective
Skeptical
Challenging

Accepting
People Focused
Empathizing
Receptive
Agreeable

C
Conscientiousness

Thoughtful
Moderate Paced
Calm
Methodical
Careful

S
Steadiness

John is a strong D with a close second score in the S category, so while he is often assertive (a D quality), he is also very accepting and agreeable (S qualities). Ryan is a strong C with a very close score in the D category. This means he is very methodical, logic-focused, skeptical, and likes to challenge information given to him (C qualities), but he's also assertive and bold (D qualities). Kate is still a little young to do the assessment at seven, but she's clearly a very strong i and, the older she gets, the more we suspect she's also a very strong D. It isn't always necessary to have people do the assessment for you to be able to identify certain personality traits.

Let's go back to Shona and Ryan's trip to the indoor playground. Now that you know a little bit about their personalities, let's examine their interaction from that perspective.

Being a strong i, Shona is people-focused, so in taking the children to the indoor playground, she's thinking about having a good time, making the kids happy, and enjoying their company. Her strong D comes into play in that she acts decisively, meaning that, in her mind, they'll all just get in the car and go. Of course she's done some planning and organizing (C qualities), which you have do to when you're a parent, but when it's time to go, it's all under control.

This is where Ryan's C qualities begin to clash with Shona. His skepticism and methodical way of approaching most things cause him to quiz Shona relentlessly on whether she has made the right arrangements or not. Does she know how to get there? Does she have enough gas in the car? Has she brought enough bottles and food for the baby? What will happen if she hasn't? It's enough to make a fun-loving, spontaneous i personality want to reach out and touch him —hard! Which is why Shona was gritting her teeth and trying not to get too frustrated. He's not trying to make her mad, he's just being himself. Using a coach approach, coupled with her knowledge of Ryan's dominant personality styles, helps her get through it without losing her temper.

You might think that having the same personality style would make it easier to get along but that's not always the case. We are fortunate in that we both have strong D qualities in our personalities, which usually means we have the same approach to decision-making (efficient) and like to move quickly through issues. Sometimes, however, this means we have a very distinct clash of wills because our D qualities tend to come with the belief that we both know the best course of action. When those courses of action differ, we clash. One thing that helps is John's secondary strength in the S style, meaning he brings a calming influence to most interactions that could escalate wildly out of control if Shona's strong i style were allowed to dominate.

We highly recommend having each of your family members over ten years of age fill out a DiSC questionnaire. You'll each receive a twenty-three page report all about you! For any children under ten, do your best to figure out where they sit on each personality style and respond accordingly using approaches that would best suit each person's style as we have described in this chapter. You might find that discussing each of your DiSC profiles is a great topic for a Family Meeting and will also add a lot of humor.

We are confident that combining your knowledge of the four DiSC personality styles with a coach approach to communication and problem-solving in your blended family will be a very powerful and useful tool. The more you can understand each other, and then respond in productive ways, the more your blended family will become a cohesive unit characterized by comfort, confidence, and, most importantly, trust.

Part 5

The Way Forward

The fact is that child rearing is a long, hard job, the rewards are not always immediately obvious, the work is undervalued, and parents are just as human and almost as vulnerable as their children.[1]

-Benjamin Spock, *Dr. Spock's Baby and Child Care,* first published in 1945

Chapter Thirteen

Thoughts for Your Journey

The family. We were a strange little band of characters trudging through life, sharing diseases and toothpaste, coveting one another's desserts, hiding shampoo, borrowing money, locking each other out of our rooms, inflicting pain and kissing to heal it in the same instant, loving, laughing, defending, and trying to figure out the common thread that bound us all together.[1]
-Erma Bombeck

By now, it's probably fairly obvious why we chose the title *Yours, Mine, and Hours* for this book. Blended families are all about combining the "yours" and "mine" and spending "hours" making it "ours." If you already live in a blended family, we're willing to bet that you saw a lot of yourselves in the stories and challenges we discussed. If you're about to become part of a blended family, we hope we haven't scared you too much! We know for sure that we haven't even scratched the surface of all the issues facing blended families, and no doubt you have some challenges we didn't even touch on.

We do hope, however, that you have found some inspiration, renewed energy, and practical approaches to dealing with the challenges you currently face or will face very soon. Life is difficult no matter what kind of family situation you live in, and the reality is that blended families simply offer the same challenges we will encounter in everyday life. The only difference is they're all rolled into one package in one place! We regularly tell our business audiences that everything we've learned about being effective leaders we've learned by living in a blended family: Effective communication, how to manage change, how to keep ourselves calm in the midst of chaos, what motivates people, conflict resolution, coaching, mentoring, setting expectations...We could go on and on but you get the picture. Blended families are merely life in miniature.

Let's go back to where we started and review the Recipe for Blended Family Success® and its three ingredients that we believe is so powerful.

Ingredient #1: Marriage

The early days of your blended family will be full of hope and positive intentions. As a couple, you are thrilled to be together and most likely have found renewal of your faith in relationships through your love and commitment to each other. We wish those days could last forever, but sooner or later reality sets in, and for blended families where children are not only instant, they're pre-existing, sooner usually means immediately. You simply don't have the luxury most new couples have of forming and building your relationship in the absence of children and interactions with ex-partners. That's why the work of putting your marriage first is so critical.

You may remember we mentioned that many people have trouble with this philosophy. We hope it's become clear to you why you simply must attend to your marriage as the primary vehicle for blended family success. Again, none of this means that your children don't take center stage in many of your priorities — they can and should. It's not a question of having to decide between your partner and your children. Our society puts too much emphasis on what we see as an artificial separation of choices. It's not about *either* your children *or* your partner — it's about *both* your children *and* your partner. Instead of either/or, it's both/and. As we keep telling seven-year-old Kate whenever a girlfriend is jealous of her spending time with another friend: the great thing about love is that there's an endless supply. There are all kinds of love in this world —love for children, for parents, for partners, for pets, for friends. Your loving one person does not in any way diminish your ability to love someone else equally. And the best part is there's always room for more.

We like to remind people that their children's job is to grow up and leave them —and your job is to help them do just that. One of the saddest things we see is couples finding themselves floundering in the space of an empty nest because they put all their time, energy, and heart into their children and give their partner only the leftovers. When we were looking for the inspirational and humorous quotes you see throughout this book, one thing that struck us was the number of quotes about marriage that are negative, cynical, and bitter. Clearly, many people are living in marriages of quiet desperation, where their dreams and goals are not only lacking support, but are actively blocked. No wonder many people pour their entire heart and soul into their children —they have no outlet for it in their partner.

Our wish for you is a loving marriage where you are free to be who you are and pursue all of your hopes and dreams. We wish you a relationship that is a sanctuary from all the trials and tribulations life will throw at you. We wish you a solid partnership that will show your children all that is possible for them when they find their own partners. As an individual and unique human being a person in your own right separate from your role as parent —you have a right to have all of these things *and* happy, healthy, well-adjusted children. You have a right to be happy in your own life.

Ingredient #2: Acceptance

The right to have your own life is one of the first things you need to accept in your blended family journey. You can beat yourself up about all the bad choices you have made in your life that now affect your children, but keep in mind that they were often the only choices you were equipped to make at the time. Instead of torturing yourself with guilt, you can put the past behind you and resolve to have a better future. I think we have offered enough research to show you that just because you got divorced or never had a partner in the picture to begin with doesn't mean that your children will be ruined forever. The regenerative power of a positive blended family for children is clear: it teaches them that bad things sometimes happen to good people, and together, you can weather the storm.

You are not going to be perfect. Neither is your partner nor your children. You can only act on things when you know about them, not before. There's a staged process in human learning[2] that goes something like this:

Stage One — Unconscious Incompetence. You aren't aware of all the things you need to know or that you even have an issue. It's difficult, if not impossible, for you to change a situation or make a different choice at this stage.

Stage Two — Conscious Incompetence. Some information or experience has come your way to highlight what you don't know. Now you're quite aware of all you need to learn. This is great because the first step in changing your life is becoming aware of what needs to change in the first place.

Stage Three — Unconscious Competence. You have now gained a lot of experience and are using your learning effectively. However, you've been working at it so long, you haven't yet realized that you've become very good at it. You don't know how much you know!

Stage Four — Conscious Competence. One day you suddenly realize how much you've learned and how much you've changed your life (and potentially your children's lives) for the better. Now you are quite aware of all that you know.

Acceptance in a blended family starts at *Stage Two* — *Conscious Incompetence*. Now that you've identified what the issues are, either in yourself or the family, you need to know it's okay that you haven't done anything about it until now. How could you have? You didn't have the skills or the awareness. You also need to know that sometimes you're not going to be able to do anything about it. This is life in a blended family: accepting there are things that need to be dealt with, that you don't and won't like it, and that some things must just be lived with because they're unresolvable.

We mentioned that you must start with reality in accepting the challenges of your blended family. It does you no good to wish things were different — they aren't. And no one is coming to save you from all of this except yourself and your partner. Many of the people you may have traditionally gone to for advice (your parents, siblings, friends) simply don't know what to do because they've never lived in a blended family themselves. While there are increasingly more resources available out there for blended families, you must still figure out a lot of things yourself. And, at the end of each day when you close the door on the world and it's just you, your partner, and your family, it's still up to you how you choose to deal with things. You can make it easier on yourself by adopting a philosophy of Acceptance, or you can spin your wheels and expend precious time and energy resisting all the difficulties.

It would be so much easier if your partner's ex wasn't in the picture. But she or he is. It would be so much easier if the kids liked you instantly. But they don't. It would be so much easier if you and your partner had the same approach to discipline. But you don't. It would be so much easier if...you fill in the blank.

Blended families aren't easy. Blended families are advanced parenting. Being a parent may be the toughest job most people will ever have, but being a stepparent is tougher. And guess what? When you signed up to be with your partner, it became your job. Never before have the words "take this job and love it" been more true.

Whatever your challenges, follow the Ten Laws of Acceptance. They're not necessarily going to change the situation, but they're going to help you change your reaction to the situation. Psychologist Carl Jung once said that the most terrifying thing in life is to accept oneself completely.[3] Acceptance doesn't mean you take only the good parts. Acceptance means you love yourself, warts and all. You truly can come to love yourself and your family, warts and all.

In the final analysis, there are no perfect families in the world. Some of the least happy families we've known are intact families that have never seen divorce. They make mistakes just like you do. You cannot shelter yourself or your children from life. Remember: most good judgment comes from experience. Most experience comes from bad judgment.

Ingredient #3: Communication

Communication is, to a large extent, about the same things Marriage and Acceptance are: a belief that we have a right to our own life and an understanding that our life will not be perfect. Setting positive personal boundaries for ourselves and taking action when they've been violated is one way to not only respect ourselves but teach our children that it's okay to respect themselves as well.

When we take responsibility for our own happiness and communicate our needs to others, that's exactly what we teach others. The future of our society truly depends on raising children who connect their choices and behavior with consequences, meaning the impact they have on others. As Doug Larson once said, "The reason people blame things on the previous generations is that there's only one other choice."[4]

Communication will always be that nagging, nebulous topic that we frequently complain about but have a hard time getting our arms around. We hope we have given you some practical tools to make sense of such a huge and complicated challenge.

The really difficult part about communication is that it's a very subjective thing because we all tend to see the world through our own unique lenses. The combination of our background, values, experiences, culture, and numerous other influences creates a filter for how we view life and the people in it. Two people can witness the same event and have a completely different account of what actually happened. It amazes us sometimes how our own siblings will have a completely different memory or interpretation of something our parents said or did, and yet all of us were there. It's like we came from a different family.

Ultimately, communication is about doing our best to ensure we have responded to people's need for information and understanding. After that, it's their choice what they do with it.

There's an old parable about two brothers who grow up with an alcoholic father. When the two brothers are adults, one becomes an alcoholic, the other doesn't. When the alcoholic brother is asked *why* he's an alcoholic, he replies, "Because my father was an alcoholic." When the non-alcoholic brother is asked why he *isn't* an alcoholic, he replies, "Because my father was an alcoholic." Same experience, different outcome.

The best thing we can do for our blended family is get out of old patterns of thinking and be open to whatever new information comes our way. Ask good, non-judgmental questions that don't assume the answer. Engage family members in dialogue and model transparent thinking to get on the same page or, at the very least, in the same book. Communication is always a work in progress, but if we had to capture the true essence of communication in one sentence, it would be this one written by Carl Buechner: "[People] may forget what you said, but they will never forget how you made them feel."[5] Wise words for any family.

Resources

www.yoursminehours.com—This is our website from which you can order additional copies of this book, download the free Family Pact planning document, and view the keynotes and workshops we have available for blended and step family events and conferences. You can also have your family complete online DiSC personality style assessments through us.

www.momentumlearning.com —Although primarily for our business/corporate clients, you can find links to all of our step parenting materials here as well.

Coaching

www.ccui.com and www.coachin.com/CoachU —Coach U is the leading global provider of coach training programs. Many coaches specialize in coaching families, and if you're interested in finding a coach to help you navigate the challenges of your blended families, you can find a coach through this website.

Communications Counsel

www.mrcom.com Mindszenthy & Roberts Communications Counsel— Gail Roberts and Bart Mindszenthy offer corporate counsel and support in major change, conflict, and crisis communications, issues management, and strategic communications planning.

Cross-Gender and Family Communications

www.georgetown/edu/faculty/tannend —This is the website of Deborah Tannen, professor of linguistics at Georgetown University. We referred in passing to her work, but this site gives you a complete listing of all of her books and publications, including some on mother/daughter communications. We highly recommend any of her work.

Money Management

The following books are all available through www.amazon.com:

Double-Income Families: Money Management for the Working Couple, by Lynne MacFarlane.

Making Allowances: A Dollars and Sense Guide to Teaching Kids About Money, by Paul W. Lermitte.

Money Habitudes for Couples, by Syble Solomon and Abby Donnelly.

Money Management for Those Who Don't Have Any, by James L. Paris.

Money Without Matrimony: The Unmarried Couple's Guide to Financial Security, by Sheryl Garrett, Debra Neiman, and Debra A. Neiman.

The Budget Kit: The Common Sense Money Management Workbook (Budget Kit), by Judy Lawrence.

The Complete Idiot's Guide to Managing Your Money (3rd Edition), by Christy Heady and Robert K. Heady.

The Financially Intelligent Parent: 8 Steps to Raising Successful, Generous, Responsible Children, by Eileen Gallo, Ph.D. and Jon Gallo, J.D.

Personality Styles

www.yoursminehours.com— Millions of people and organizations worldwide have gained insight about themselves and others through the DiSC® learning instruments pioneered over thirty years ago by Inscape Publishing. Shona and John hold a license to deliver the *Everything DiSC* materials in workshop format, including ordering and administering online questionnaires through this website.

Step parenting and Blended Families

The following books are all available on www.amazon.com:

The Smart Stepfamily: New Seven Steps to a Healthy Family, by Ron L. Deal.

Stepcoupling. Creating and Sustaining a Strong Marriage in Today's Blended Family, by Susan Wisdom and Jennifer Green.

The Enlightened Stepmother: Revolutionizing the Role, by Perdita K. Norwood and Teri Winender.

7 Steps to Bonding With Your Stepchild, by Suzen J. Ziegahn.

The Blended Family Sourcebook: A Guide to Negotiating Change, by David S. Chedekel and Karen O'Connell.

The following books are references we found particularly helpful and affirming. We found them in our local bookstore:

Stepfamilies: Love, Marriage and Parenting in the First Decade, by Dr. James H. Bray and John Kelly. 1998. New York: Broadway Books.

The Complete Idiot's Guide to Stepparenting, by Ericka Lutz. 1998. Indianapolis: Alpha Books.

The Stepparent's Survival Guide: A Workbook for Creating a Happy Blended Family, by Suzen J. Ziegahn, Ph.D. 2002. Oakland: New Harbinger Publications Inc.

The following organizations and publications provide numerous resources and support for people living in step and blended families:

www.blended-families.com —Monthly newsletters and tele-classes.

www.bonusfamilies.com —How to build and maintain healthy relationships and nurturing support systems after divorce and separation. Discussion forums for teens living in step and blended families.

www.comamas.com —A great site examining how step moms and biological moms can work together for everyone's best interests. It was developed by two co-mamas who worked things out and are now sharing their strategies.

www.istepfamily.com —The official 24/7 online support group of the International Stepfamily Foundation.

www.stepfamilies.info —This is the website of the National Stepfamily Resource Center. The center's primary objective is to serve as a clearinghouse for information, resources, and support for stepfamily members and the professionals who work with them.

www.stepfamily.ca —The website of the Stepfamily Foundation of Alberta offers a comprehensive list of how-to articles on a multitude of issues related to step parenting.

www.stepfamily.org —Articles and downloadable e-booklets for answers to many step parenting questions.

www.stepfamilymagazine.com —An online step family magazine.

www.yourstepfamily.com —*Your Stepfamily* is owned by YSF LLC and is a privately held, women-owned publishing company producing educational magazines and trade show publications. With the premiere issue published in Q3 2002, *Your Stepfamily* became the first magazine dedicated to addressing the changes and challenges faced by millions of stepfamilies. Each issue provides realistic practices and tips that stepfamilies can employ to strengthen family members from within. *Your Stepfamily* is the official magazine of the Stepfamily Association of America, and a portion of each subscription goes to the association. For more information, visit: www.yourstepfamily.com or call 847.462.5783.

Chapter References

Prologue

[1]http://parenthood.library.wisc.edu/Bliss/Bliss.html — Statistics and advice pages on step parenting by Beverly Bliss, Ph.D. and www12.statcan.ca/English/census01/ products/analytic/companion/fam/Canada.cfm

Part 1

[1] www.quoteland.com

Chapter One

[1]www.quotationspage.com

[2] 1998. Bray, Dr. James H. and Kelly, John. *Step Families: Love, marriage, and parenting in the first decade.* New York: Broadway Books, p. 12.

Part 2

[1]www.samueljohnson.com

Chapter Two

[1]www.brainyquote.com

[2] 1998. Bray, Dr. James H. and Kelly, John. *Step Families: Love,*

marriage, and parenting in the first decade. New York: Broadway Books, p. 23.

[3] www.wmbridges.com

[4] 1998. Bray, Dr. James H. and Kelly, John. *Step Families: Love, marriage, and parenting in the first decade.* New York: Broadway Books, p. 42.

Chapter Three

[1] www.brainyquote.com

[2] www.marriagemissions.com

[3] http://healthresources.caremark.com/topic/emptynests

[4] http://thinkexist.com/quotes

[5] http://clubs.yahoo.com/clubs/adultkidsofdivorce

[6] www.brainyquote.com

Chapter Four

[1] www.brainyquote.com

[2] 1998. Bray, Dr. James H. and Kelly, John. *Step Families: Love, marriage, and parenting in the first decade.* New York: Broadway Books, p. 13.

[3] http://marriage.about.com/cs/sexualstatistics/a/sexstatistics.htm

Chapter Five

[1] www.famous-quotes-and-quotations.com/marriage-quotes.html

Part 3

[1] http://thinkexist.com/quotes

Chapter Six

[1] www.brainyquote.com

[2] Thoughts shared with Shona by Dr. Susan Hutton, former professor at the University of Calgary.

Chapter Seven

[1] www.brainyquote.com

[2] 1994. Senge, Peter M. et al. *The Fifth Discipline Fieldbook: Strategies and tools for building a learning organization.* New York: Currency, p. 109. We actually learned about this technique long before we read Senge's book from our colleagues in the construction industry who regularly use the Five Whys approach in identifying root causes of safety incidents. Senge notes that this exercise is partly based on an established Japanese quality technique and its description by quality consultant Peter Scholtes. It appears this technique exists in the public domain now.

Chapter Eight

[1] http://thinkexist.com/quotes

Part 4

[1] www.elise.com/quotes

Chapter Nine

[1] www.wisdomquotes.com

[2] 1994. Tannen, Deborah. *Talking from 9 to 5: How Women's and Men's Conversational Styles Affect Who Gets Heard, Who Gets Credit, and What Gets Done at Work.* New York: William Morrow and Company Inc.

[3] 1994. Tannen, Deborah. *Talking from 9 to 5: How Women's and Men's Conversational Styles Affect Who Gets Heard, Who Gets Credit, and What Gets Done at Work.* New York: William Morrow and Company Inc.

Chapter Ten

[1] www.wisdomquotes.com

[2] www.mrcom.com is the best place to get in touch with Gail Roberts and Bart Mindszenthy.

[3] en.wikipedia.org/wiki/Maslow's_hierarchy_of_needs

Chapter Eleven

[1] www.wisdomquotes.com

Chapter Twelve

[1] www.brainyquote.com

[2] www.ccui.com/CoachU/ — Shona attended Corporate Coach U as part of her licensing process to facilitate the program *The Coaching Clinic.* Some elements in Chapter Twelve come directly from that program, including the concepts of *Asking Thought-Provoking Questions,* parts of *Becoming Comfortable With Silence,* and the *80-20* rule under *Talk Less and Listen More.*

[3] www.inscapepublishing.com — Shona and John hold a license to deliver the *Everything DiSC®* materials in workshop format, including ordering and administering online questionnaires.

See our websites at www.yoursminehours.com and www. momentumlearning.com.

Part 5

[1] www.quoteland.com

Chapter Thirteen

[1] www.quotegarden.com

[2] www.businessballs.com/consciouscompetencelearningmodel. htm

[3] en.wikiquote.org

[4] www.brainyquote.com

[5] http://thinkexist.com/quotes

About the Authors

Shona Welsh and John Penton have lived together in a blended family of five children, one puppy, and the occasional mouse for the past nine years.

The winner of numerous writing and speaking awards, Shona Welsh is the author of *Mentoring the Future: A Guide to Building Mentor Programs that Work* and coauthor of the best-selling *Expert Women Who Speak: Speak Out, Volume 6*. Shona holds a master's degree in adult education and has been speaking internationally on work and life issues for the past twenty years. She cannot be left alone in the house with chocolate.

John Penton has had various incarnations as a carpenter, farmer, teacher, and gravedigger. Most recently, he has been speaking on numerous parenting issues to a variety of audiences. A certified family mediator with a background in child development, John holds a master's degree in education and is the author of *Big Boys Don't Cry: The Suppression of Male Nurture in Teaching and Learning*. He keeps a stash of chocolate under the bed he thinks Shona doesn't know about.

Together, Shona and John operate a personal development and business training organization called Momentum Learning Inc.

To contact Shona and John:
www.yoursminehours.com

or

www.momentumlearning.com
Phone: 403-932-8882
shona.welsh@momentumlearning.com
john.penton@momentumlearning.com

Made in the USA